COPING SUCCESSFULLY WITH
YOUR SECOND CHILD

FIONA MARSHALL has wide writing experience as a journalist in London and Mexico City and has contributed many articles to parenting magazines. She lives in south-west London with her husband and young family – this book was written after the birth of her own second child.

GW00319629

Overcoming Common Problems Series

For a full list of titles please contact
Sheldon Press, Marylebone Road, London NW1 4DU

Beating Job Burnout
DR DONALD SCOTT

Beating the Blues
SUSAN TANNER AND JILLIAN
BALL

Being the Boss
STEPHEN FITZSIMON

Birth Over Thirty
SHEILA KITZINGER

Body Language
How to read others' thoughts by their
gestures
ALLAN PEASE

Bodypower
DR VERNON COLEMAN

Bodysense
DR VERNON COLEMAN

Calm Down
How to cope with frustration and anger
DR PAUL HAUCK

Changing Course
How to take charge of your career
SUE DYSON AND STEPHEN HOARE

Comfort for Depression
JANET HORWOOD

Complete Public Speaker
GYLES BRANDRETH

**Coping Successfully with Your Child's
Asthma**
DR PAUL CARSON

**Coping Successfully with Your Hyperactive
Child**
DR PAUL CARSON

**Coping Successfully with Your Irritable
Bowel**
ROSEMARY NICOL

Coping with Anxiety and Depression
SHIRLEY TRICKETT

Coping with Blushing
DR ROBERT EDELMANN

Coping with Cot Death
SARAH MURPHY

Coping with Depression and Elation
DR PATRICK McKEON

Coping with Stress
DR GEORGIA WITKIN-LANOIL

Coping with Suicide
DR DONALD SCOTT

Coping with Thrush
CAROLINE CLAYTON

Curing Arthritis – The Drug-Free Way
MARGARET HILLS

Curing Arthritis Diet Book
MARGARET HILLS

**Curing Coughs, Colds and Flu – The
Drug-Free Way**
MARGARET HILLS

Curing Illness – The Drug-Free Way
MARGARET HILLS

Depression
DR PAUL HAUCK

Divorce and Separation
ANGELA WILLANS

Don't Blame Me!
How to stop blaming yourself
and other people
TONY GOUGH

The Epilepsy Handbook
SHELAGH McGOVERN

**Everything You Need to Know about
Adoption**
MAGGIE JONES

**Everything You Need to Know about
Contact Lenses**
DR ROBERT YOUNGSON

**Everything You Need to Know about
Osteoporosis**
ROSEMARY NICOL

Overcoming Common Problems Series

Overcoming Common Problems Series

Overcoming Common Problems

COPING SUCCESSFULLY
WITH YOUR SECOND
CHILD

Fiona Marshall

SHELDON PRESS
LONDON

First published in Great Britain in 1992
Sheldon Press, SPCK, Marylebone Road, London NW1 4DU

British Library Cataloguing in Publication Data
Marshall, Fiona
    Coping successfully with your second child.
    1.
    I. Title
    649.122

    ISBN 0–85969–635–9

Photoset by Deltatype Ltd, Ellesmere Port, Cheshire
Printed in Great Britain by Biddles Ltd, Guildford and Kings Lynn

Contents

Introduction

Second baby, second nature?

First children get all the frills: they get the pristine lace on the Moses basket, and untouched fluffy teddies with both eyes sewn on straight; they get beautifully illustrated baby dictionaries – and, it is said, they learn to read sooner and faster than the siblings who follow them. First babies are also said to do better in terms of parental attention, and they don't do so badly when it comes to the next door neighbour, your mother-in-law or even your crusty old aunt, either. Everyone loves a first baby! And so they should. But second babies, though they may be equally adored, often don't get the same star treatment (except perhaps from discerning grand-parents). There just isn't the time or energy. Pregnancy, birth and afterwards have to be slotted in to an already demanding lifestyle.

Most parents of one child consider a second child at some point, even if they eventually decide to rest content with one. After all, once you have one, you might as well have two, surely? You've got all the babygros and the experience left over from the first; two can't be more trouble to look after than one; besides, Junior needs company. Or so the reasoning goes. Isn't a second baby just something that mothers have sooner *or* later? Well, not quite. In the event, a second baby can shatter your lifestyle quite as effectively as a first. In this age of the one (designer) child, a second baby can be something of a rude awakening – for parents and toddlers alike! Suddenly there's less time for the adored first child; there's more pressure and less freedom to work just when income is most needed. Just when the toddler's getting on his feet, you're suddenly thrown back a couple of years or so, tied once again by a new baby. The cosy family unit meets a major life crisis.

This book aims to explore that crisis in as positive a way as possible, and to offer the information and support that will help meet the challenges of second-time parenthood. It would be unrealistic to deny that a second baby can bring specific problems and pressures, but it is hoped that these can be worked through more easily with the benefit of other people's experience. Any situation is easier to cope with if you can read about someone else in the same position!

When expecting my own second baby, I hunted in vain for some extensive, comforting manual that would help lead me through my own foray into the unknown. After being deluged with printed material throughout a first pregnancy, it came as a bit of a shock to realize that, as far as the written word was concerned, I was more or less alone. Although most baby books offered bits of information, nothing I read told me, in depth, what it was *really* like to have a second baby; that was something I had to learn for myself!

Having a second baby *is* different from having a first. It isn't that another baby represents an extra 50 per cent more work: it's that he or she brings a complete change of lifestyle. This can be difficult for parents to imagine in advance because they consider themselves to be already broken in to parenthood! One child engendered such massive adjustments that they can't imagine more change would be demanded with another; it has to be easier second time round. Yes, it can be easier in that you know what to do – breastfeeding, changing, night wakings, may not be the headache they were first time round – but it's the fact that the whole momentum of life changes, just as it did with the birth of a first baby. This time, both parents are that much more committed to having a family; some would even say, burdened. Second-time parents can feel even more alone than first-timers – deemed worthy of only a few token pages by standard baby books and treated as an old hand by the medical profession and friends, and without the novelty and excitement of the first. And, as time goes on, the demands of *two* small children can lead to increasing social isolation for the parents.

Practicalities also have to be sorted out, such as where the new baby will sleep, whether the children will wake each other at night, and how to breastfeed with a demanding toddler at your elbow. Some families find the upheaval lasts a couple of months; others are still struggling one year on.

Whether you're thinking about another baby, are pregnant, or have recently given birth again, you will find there are adjustments to be made with the advent of a second child. Of course it isn't all bad news: the miracle of birth is no less a miracle second time round, and another person in your life remains a fantastic privilege. The second time too, you're likely to be more relaxed; you may even enjoy your baby more! But if more conscious preparation were made for the birth of a second baby, the arrival of this new person wouldn't be such a shock to the family's existing dynamic.

In addition to drawing on my own experience, I consulted several couples while this book was in progress: this was the experience of one of them, Laura, a teacher, mother of Henry, two, and baby Alicia:

> I had the perfect second baby: she slept well and fed well, was easily comforted, and hardly ever cried. Nevertheless, it was just such a shock to have another person around. You'd think you'd be prepared, having had one baby, but it isn't like that. Life with a toddler was so busy, I didn't give that much thought to the new baby while I was pregnant – I assumed that there was nothing to having a second baby, that she would just fit in. No one warns you that having a second baby is like having a first in terms of shock. Suddenly it feels as if you have four children, not two! Our routine was completely turned on its head for about a year.

Having a second child does inevitably raise different issues from the first time round. Although you want another child, the excitement this time may well be tinged with more sober reflections. You'll probably be more aware of the responsibility; and perhaps thoughtful about the cost. It's not that children themselves are that expensive to begin with, it's just that they stop both parents working unless they can afford the childcare (which still has to be paid for). You also know how demanding just one small child can be. There are bound to be one or two (maybe more) inner groans at the thought of the baby turmoil ahead – the broken nights, the flung food, the crying and the mess. All this added to that new unknown quantity, your toddler!

When considering your first pregnancy, there were only two people to bear in mind: you and your partner. Now there's a third – your first child. You want to provide company for him, but will he appreciate it or will he be jealous? And can you bear to let him go just yet? How will you manage with two when one is such a handful sometimes? Will there be any time left over for anything else?

Well, it has certainly been done before, but nevertheless having a second baby may bring some changes in lifestyle which you didn't perhaps anticipate. For example, you may suddenly realize that the childminder's fees will double. This may mean you decide to give up work rather than pay most of your wages to the childminder. This in turn will mean you will have to trim your spending because there's no longer a second salary around for new clothes and holidays abroad. Alternatively, maybe your partner gets a better-paid job which involves moving house; or maybe you move anyway because the house suddenly feels too small.

There are also the adjustments you may need to make in your image of yourself. One child can to a large extent be tucked into your normal activities – swimming, visiting friends, shopping, visiting exhibitions, working. But all these become far more difficult with another child around. With two, you're much more likely to feel yourself branded 'mother'!

Equally daunting can be the sheer upheaval of another pregnancy again, with all the rigours of morning sickness, ante-natal appointments and general exhaustion. Although it's all easier because you know what to expect, it's also harder because you have all the extra work of looking after your first child as well. However, experience does mean you should be more confident. What's more, the chances are you'll have an easier, shorter birth. Whereas first labours last on average for 12 hours, you might just get away with a mere seven or so second time round!

One question many mothers ask themselves is whether they'll be able to love another baby in the same way as they do the first. Rest assured, the human heart is expandable, and can easily take in another child. The balance of your relationship with your first will alter – but this happens anyway, as she gets bigger and more independent. Your relationship with your first child *is* special – but so will be your relationship with your second, even if you can't imagine this right now. Each child will build his or her individual links of love with you.

Note: With regard to the sexes of the children, the toddler is designated 'he' and 'she' in alternate chapters (except when specific examples are being referred to); and, for clarity, the baby is always the opposite sex to the toddler. Also, in default of other vocabulary, 'toddler' is used as a catch-all word for the elder child.

1

The Second Pregnancy

Congratulations, you're pregnant again! How do you feel? Excited? Nervous? Wondering what you've let yourself in for? Don't worry. Thousands have done the same and survived to tell the tale! This book is the distilled experience of some of them, passed on in the hope that it may make life a little easier for those who are contemplating or embarking on having a second child. As you'll see, though there may be no truth in the myth that two children are easier to look after than one, no one has yet tried to prove that life with two is less interesting or less rich! In fact, two children *can* be easier than just one, because they will play together sooner and so not bother you as much – but that comes later, when the younger child can walk and talk and generally fend for himself. First there's two to three years or more, during which you have to get through the pregnancy and the early stages of life with two, and this book is designed to help you do just that. And of course it all starts with the pregnancy – and before.

The decision

Why have a second baby? For many first-time parents, it's a deceptively easy decision to make, one which they slide into naturally: to give their first child company, to make a 'real' family. Once you've spent a year or so living amid the welter of bitten toys and grubby walls one baby generates, you become case-hardened.

Hilda, who worked part-time as a geriatric nurse, had two children. Toby was just over two when Ben arrived:

> I always knew we would have two, and have them quickly. Having a first baby is such a massive adaptation that you feel you'd better have a second while you're still in that frame of mind! I feel if I'd left it too long, I might not have bothered. But of course our main reason for going ahead was that we wanted a brother or sister for Toby.

Apart from that powerful, little-understood urge in us towards new

5

life, providing company for the existing child is one of the commonest reasons given for having a second child. Whenever you produce the 'two's company' argument, however, there's always some sunbeam ready to pop up and declare how badly she and her sister got on in their young days, or how dreadfully her own children fight. This is likely to be true some of the time, but it would be a shame to let such people put a damper on your enthusiasm for new life with their negativity!

Thanks to the drop in infant mortality over the last century, we no longer need to have many children in order to replace ourselves. Nevertheless, perhaps part of the underlying reason for having a second child is a fear of investing too much emotionally in an only child, both for her sake and ours; a feeling that it is healthier and more generous to go ahead with another child.

Some people have an uneasy feeling about an only child – that she'll be lonely, or, worse, spoiled. Of course this doesn't have to be so, and some couples feel an only child is right for them because of their individual ability to give time, love and financial security to their offspring. For example, only children often do better academically than their peers, partly because they have a larger share of their parents' attention, partly because there is more money to spend on education. The decision is of course influenced by social structures. In Victorian times, the decision to have a second baby was no more momentous than the one to have a third or a fourth. In today's Britain, two children remains a constant favourite family number for children (well, 1.8 if you can bear to think of statisticians dividing your children for their convenience). More people have two babies than any other number (around 40 per cent as opposed to just 14 per cent for one, and 20 per cent for three).

So, can we really realize the implications of a second pregnancy before we decide to go ahead? For most mothers, memories of the first pregnancy and birth are alive enough to make them think seriously before plunging in again. It's a different matter to sally forth boldly into the unknown with a first child, and to repeat a long, sometimes hard, familiar haul – the 40 weeks of pregnancy, the birth, those first confused weeks, and the gradual evolving of a routine which could be likened to carving a sculpture out of hard stone.

Most women, then, know that having a second child will be a diminution of their freedom – or do they?

Mother of Henry, two, and baby Alicia, Laura, a teacher, puts it quite bluntly:

> Actually, you don't realise how well off you are with just one. What an easy life I had! Transport, going out, everything was so much easier! Henry was just 15 months old when I went ahead with a second pregnancy. Looking back, I don't know how I had the nerve! It seems to me that I didn't think about it at all, but of course I did. It's just that you have no idea what it's going to be like – chiefly never having any time to yourself, being sick, being tired, all with a demanding toddler around.

It seems we don't have babies for the ease of body or soul they give: parents perforce rise above such matters, though most second-time mothers probably wouldn't articulate it quite like that. Laura struggles to explain the drive towards bigger-heartedness:

> Yes, I did know that going ahead with a second pregnancy wouldn't be all roses – but I suppose that isn't what it's all about.

Planning and preparation

But just how far can you plan a second pregnancy anyway? Some people take it for granted they will have a second child and have no difficulty conceiving. Indeed, getting pregnant may happen rather sooner than expected, and is a common feature of the second pregnancy because, with another child in mind at some point, couples may be less careful than they might be about interim contraception. Other people, however, can face a wait of a year or more before becoming pregnant again. Even in these days of effective birth control, planning can't be perfect. It's a sad fact that 50 per cent of infertility relates to women who have been pregnant before; some women don't go on to have a second baby because they can't.

Mind the gap!

As you might guess, there's no perfect age gap between children, though it is worth bearing some points in mind.

The most common debate is between a two- and three-year gap.

If your toddler is two when the new baby arrives, however grown up she appears to you now, she does in fact still need you quite a lot, both physically and psychologically. She'll still be needing a pushchair at times, and nappies at least at night; she's bound also to want lifting and carrying. What's more she may be in the throes of the 'terrible twos', and will need you to sort out her tantrums; she will also want you to read to her, cuddle her, and generally mother her. In many ways, the two-year-old is still a baby in her dependence.

However, although the initial period may be harder work for you, the children will play together sooner and so be far less work for you. This playing together starts at around 9–10 months, becomes established around 16–18 months, and is blossoming nicely by the time your youngest is around two (though obviously you still have to keep an eye on them.) The two-year-old is also more likely to forget any jealousy more quickly, and to integrate the baby into her life sooner. Siblings who grow up with a close gap may well remain closer throughout life.

A three-year gap can mean a much easier life for you. You'll be able to spend whole hours of your pregnancy with your feet up with a book while your child trots off to playschool. After the birth, you may escape much of the desperation of mothers who have two under-3-year-olds with the frantic strain involved in looking after two small, demanding children. Perhaps the best aspect of the three-year gap is that you can give your first child all your attention while she still needs so much of it. On the other hand, an older, more aware child may take longer to adapt, and she may be more jealous – though it's by no means guaranteed.

A bigger gap still may mean your first child is at school, so that you will have a good part of the day free to care for the baby. Here it's worthwhile considering the implications of the gap for you. With two small children close together, you do 'get it over with,' to use a common if ungracious phrase of many mothers. It can be hard returning to babycare after a longer break and losing your independence and perhaps your ability to work again. The whole family will be that much more used to being a three-person unit. On the other hand, you may be more financially secure; and, an older child will be less physical trouble to care for – and may even be able to help you a little!

8

Looking after yourself

It is worth putting extra thought into a second pregnancy. Looking after one child is tiring, especially if you work outside the house as well, and ideally you need to be in good physical condition before undertaking another pregnancy. Some doctors even say you should start improving your health nine months before trying to conceive. Don't forget that your partner needs to look after himself, too, so that his sperm are as healthy as possible. So just what can you do? No doubt you remember these guidelines from your first pregnancy, but they may well be more difficult to achieve this time round because you are so busy. They remain just as important, though.

Diet

Good nutrition is one of the key factors in a healthy pregnancy. Follow the healthy eating guidelines: less sugar, salt and fat, more fresh fruit and vegetables; plenty of wholegrain products; protein in the form of white meat, fish (white and oily), cheese, nuts and pulses. It isn't a question of cooking elaborate meals: even the busiest mother can throw together a healthy snack lunch of cheese, wholemeal bread and a raw vegetable salad – which is good for your toddler as well as you!

Smoking

Smoking contributes to infertility, is more likely to cause miscarriage, limits your baby's growth, and is more likely to cause congenital malformation such as hare lip and cleft palate. Passive smoking is also bad for your toddler. If you had trouble giving up during your first pregnancy, don't despair, but do try and take alternative action. A second pregnancy can be more of a strain than the first, and you do need extra escape routes. Explore other ways of treating yourself or relaxing; find friends to give you moral support; and take a short view of life – no more than the next three hours – and see if you can manage without a cigarette for that long. When your toddler makes you feel you must have one, go into another room and scream! If you really can't give up, cut down to less than ten a day; or for the Health Education Authority leaflet, How to Give Up Smoking For You and Your Baby, contact your district health authority.

Drinking

There are days with a small child when a gin and tonic around bath time seems the only answer. However it's only comparatively recently that doctors have realized there is no safe limit for alcohol consumption in pregnancy. Alcohol does the most damage in the early weeks of pregnancy, especially weeks 6 to 12, so it's a good idea to cut it out before you try and conceive. Instead of pouring yourself a drink at bathtime, try something different: get into the bath with your child and relax that way, or lie in her bed together and listen to some music for ten minutes. Treat yourself later to alcohol-free wine or beer with your partner.

If you don't conceive

You've probably heard stories of women who gave up trying for a child in order to adopt – only to find themselves pregnant – and some researchers have believed that at least 50 per cent of infertility is 'all in the mind'. While the latest research indicates that in fact psychological problems don't cause infertility, do try and maintain a relaxed approach if you fail to conceive as soon as you hoped. A year's wait for a second child is by no means unusual. If you want more help, you might find a book useful (see Bibliography); you can also contact your doctor or a support group (see Addresses).

Post-natal sexual problems

Sometimes another pregnancy may be delayed by sexual problems stemming from the birth of the first child. For some unfortunate people, discomfort from stitches or an episiotomy can last for many months, making sex painful or impossible. An inflammation or fibroid tumour can also cause pain, as can prolapse of the uterus (when the tip of the uterus drops into the vagina). This common problem can take months or years to develop and can be traced back to the birth or just after. (Strict use of pelvic floor exercises can correct this, or surgery if it's too far gone.)

Lack of interest or low sex drive can also hinder a return to active sex life. This often follows a difficult birth, because of fatigue or for other psychosexual reasons. Poor contraception can also lead to a habit of not having sex which then makes it hard to conceive when you want to later on; a poorly-fitting contraceptive cap, or the wrong type of pill, which causes uncomfortable breakthrough bleeding can be, quite literally, a turn-off.

The child as contraceptive is a well-known issue to many parents! It's not so much a matter of the little face peeping round the door at the wrong time as the simple fact of exhaustion. After a trying day with a small person, the only further contact you're likely to want from your partner is a chaste cuddle. In practice, however, this often means that opportunities for sex are reduced, rather than cut out altogether.

If you are worried, consult your doctor, to determine whether any difficulty is due to physical causes. Otherwise, it may be worth contacting a marriage guidance counsellor (see Addresses).

The pregnancy: your reactions

Being pregnant again gives you a second chance – a chance to appreciate it all in a way that perhaps wasn't possible first time round. A first pregnancy can easily be spent anxiously attending to symptoms – nausea, heartburn, backache – and the pangs which might or might not be labour. This time, it's easier to float with the tide; to revel in the new life growing within you. You might find you want to keep this pregnancy to yourself for a while longer before you tell the outside world; in some ways, a second child is yours the way a first one isn't. What with excited grandparents-to-be and interested friends, a first baby becomes public property quickly.

But there should be room for other reactions, too: grief at once again saying goodbye to the known and familiar, at leaving behind another portion of your life and at letting your first baby go. Some women feel a dismayed kind of *déja-vu* at being pregnant again, and it feels too soon to go through it all again. There are fears, too. How will I cope? Why have I tied myself down again? It's natural to feel ambivalence and even depression. Also don't forget the major hormonal changes taking place in your body can play havoc with your moods. If you find you do get depressed, try one or more of the following:

- Find someone to talk to honestly who won't judge you.
- Try and let the mood pass – don't analyse it all endlessly as hormonal changes may make you feel different tomorrow!
- Look after your self-image, even in small ways: a new hair clip, a scarf, a large bow to pin to a dress, some skin cream.
- Discuss specific anxieties about the pregnancy and birth with a qualified, competent person – your doctor or midwife.

11

Will it be different?

Pregnancies can vary enormously in the same person. For example, many mothers report feeling less sick during a second pregnancy, perhaps because the body is more accustomed to being pregnant, or simply because they have less time to think about it! You have the advantage of knowing what pregnancy is like, but even so, you can't really know how this one will go. There *is* a general tendency for a second pregnancy to show sooner because your abdominal muscles have already been stretched. Otherwise, perhaps the main problems in a second pregnancy are never having time to yourself, and feeling extra tired (see p. 14 on Rest).

Pregnancy after previous problems

It can take courage to become pregnant again if it wasn't all straightforward last time round, and how you view the pregnancy and birth will of course be conditioned by your first experience.

Although she wanted a second child, Penny, a librarian, frankly dreaded her second birth. Her first pregnancy had gone normally but had ended without warning in an abruption of the placenta, when heavy haemorrhaging resulted in an emergency Caesarean in order to save her baby. No one could explain why this had happened to Penny, and both she and her husband Robert, an insurance broker, felt increasingly nervous as the expected delivery date approached. In the event, Penny was able to have a normal second delivery, though, she says: 'I wish I'd been able to relax more and be more positive about it – I'm sure the fear made it all more painful than it need have been'.

If your first birth didn't go as you'd hoped, it can be difficult to avoid feelings of fear, anger and sorrow. But do try and leave room for change – it may be easier this time round. Obviously, you can't guarantee the birth will go well, but you can use the time to prepare yourself. There may be something extra you could do to boost your morale: yoga classes, perhaps, or a study of a few pregnancy books. Talking can also help: try your friends, or contact the National Childbirth Trust or MAMA (Meet-a-Mum Association, see Addresses).

Problems or not, do be ruthless about accepting any help offered, from your partner, family or friends. Don't be a martyr! If you did have problems last time, you'll need to discuss your individual case with your doctor or midwife, but here's what to expect as a rough guide if you have had:

Pre-eclampsia

A condition characterized by high blood pressure, pre-eclamptic toxaemia (PET) has no known cause though it is more common in first pregnancies. If you *did* have it in your first pregnancy there is a 1 in 10 chance of getting it again, though there is no way of telling whether or not you will be unlucky this time. As it has been associated with poor nutrition, you can make sure you eat really well, being especially careful to have enough protein.

Pre-eclampsia doesn't normally occur before the 20th week of pregnancy and regular antenatal checks will monitor any possible signs – protein in the urine, oedema (swelling in feet, hands, or face from fluid) or excessive weight gain.

Previous Caesarean

Although doctors may mutter from time to time about your scar rupturing during labour, their concern is largely academic, as rupture of a previous scar only occurs in around 0.1 per cent of pregnancies (some doctors say even less). Your medical advisers will reserve the right to perform another Caesarean if necessary, often with a 'trial of labour' first – that is, labour is allowed to proceed naturally to see how things progress, with the proviso that an operation will be performed if necessary.

Whether you'll have a second Caesarean does depend on why you had one the first time. Some conditions are 'one-offs' – placenta praevia, for example, when the placenta blocks the cervix and therefore the baby's exit. In other cases, a doctor can tell you from the start of the pregnancy that another operation will be necessary –for example, if your pelvis is too narrow for a vaginal birth (cephalo-pelvic disproportion) or if you suffer from a condition such as diabetes or heart trouble.

Previous miscarriage

Miscarriage is extremely common and is Nature's way of dealing with defects. First pregnancies are more likely to miscarry than later ones. In fact, about a third of all first pregnancies miscarry. If you have ever miscarried it's unlikely that it will happen again, unless

13

you have any contributing medical condition. You can try for another baby as soon as you feel like it.

Other conditions likely to cause miscarriage

You will need medical attention in your pregnancy if you have:

Incompetent cervix: the neck of the womb gapes between weeks 14 and 20, aborting the fetus. This can be treated by a small stitch in the cervix which is removed when labour starts.

Fibroids in the uterus: these benign tumours may need to be removed by an operation before successful pregnancy can take place.

Immune resistance: Your uterus rejects the growing baby as a 'foreign body'. This is treated by innoculation with your partner's blood cells.

The mechanics of rest

Those were the days, first-time round, when you had time to put your feet up in the afternoon and browse through a book of baby names! Now, you'll be lucky if you get a chance to sit down for five minutes, never mind the suggested one or two hours rest a day. As with other aspects of self-care, however, rest is just as vital as before, if more elusive! If you have a child at playgroup or nursery for part of the week, your only difficulty will be to discipline yourself to rest instead of shopping, tidying and other useful chores.

Here are a few ideas to get your toddler to rest so that you can, too:

- Make the most of those times when your toddler is napping. This sounds obvious, but too many of us rush off to cook dinner the minute we get a bit of peace!
- See if you can interest her in quiet, sit-down pursuits, such as modelling dough, playing with dolls or drawing on your lap.
- Get your partner to take care of her at weekends so you can catch up on sleep, too. Book him in advance if need be!
- Give her a long, splashy, bubbly bath – any time. Bring a comfortable chair and book into the bathroom for yourself.
- Get into your bed together for a cuddle and rest.
- Wheel her out in her pushchair to see if she'll sleep.

- Listen to children's radio or a cassette together.

However you grab your rest, make some time for your growing baby. All too often during a second pregnancy there just isn't the time to think about him, and you may feel sad and guilty about this. So, make yourself comfortable in a chair or on a bed, prop yourself up with a few pillows, and spend time focusing on your baby.

Your mind needs recreation, too. At some point during a second pregnancy it becomes easy to feel that life is rather circumscribed, especially if you've been looking after your first baby at home. Recharge your psychic batteries with whatever suits you: some temporary work, paid or voluntary; a watercolour class; a new course of reading.

Parentcraft classes again?

You may not want to bother with a whole course of ante-natal classes again, especially if it means finding someone to mind your child. Some hospitals do offer one or more refresher classes for parents, or you could try something different, like an NCT or Active Birth class. Do take advantage of the usual hospital tour and have a good look at the labour ward, even if it is the same one, just to boost your confidence. And, don't forget that classes can be useful for meeting other mothers – something that may be more difficult after the birth.

A break before the birth?

Do it! Not only will it be good for you, it will give your child a useful practice run for the time you'll be away in hospital, unless you're opting for a home birth.

Organizing a weekend away can seem like more trouble than it's worth, but it does give you time with yourself and your partner – a rare commodity after the birth of a second. Plan something alone, even, or with your partner or a friend – a retreat, a hobby weekend, or just a night away.

2

Preparing Your Toddler

When it comes to preparing your toddler, you may perhaps feel that it's already too late. Perhaps the baby is already with you and you feel that toddler jealousy is an inescapable fact of life. Or maybe you feel that you all got off to an awkward start and there isn't much that can be done about it, but, as you'll rapidly learn if you haven't already done so, second-time parenthood is no time for perfection. You may have had the time and energy first time round to put your ideals into action (no chocolate biscuits or smacking) but with two children it's a fact that you can't always live as you'd like! This applies no less to preparing your toddler. The birth may have come and gone, or you may still be waiting. Either way, you can try and help your first child, both now and in the future. Small children can do with their mothers' support any time.

A difficult time ahead?

Preparing your first child for the birth of the second is probably the most dreaded of the tasks faced by second-time mothers. But why introduce the 'green-eyed monster' before you need to? We all know that even the bolshiest of toddlers is a highly suggestible beast, so don't even whisper the word jealousy when the chances are that he may not yet have thought of it! A small child takes his cue from his parents, and tends to live up – or down – to their expectations.

Jealousy may develop much later than you expect, in the form of rivalry for the parents' attention once the baby is bigger and more mobile. Of course, your toddler may simply be jealous from the start: someone else *has* arrived to share all the love and attention which used to be exclusively his. However, adequate preparation and assurances of your love can still cut down on the possibility of this happening. In fact, many children are not jealous when a new baby arrives – intrigued and unsettled would perhaps be nearer the mark. The visits to the hospital, the presents and the excitement, may all delay the reality sinking in for a while. In addition, as tiny babies lead a relatively restricted life, they don't – from the

16

toddler's viewpoint – actually do that much which can create jealousy.

What is just as likely to disturb the toddler is 1. the knowledge during your pregnancy that something big but vague is going on and 2. the change in his routine occasioned by the birth and afterwards. Creatures of habit as most small children are, they're more likely to be bothered by the new, little-understood, emotional atmosphere in the house, and the disruption of the normal flow of events.

For now, you can take the pressure off your toddler first by explaining what is going on in terminology that he can understand, and second, by accepting that change – any change – has to be part of his lifestyle. No matter how secure your first child's routine is, life will throw up other landmarks – for example, starting nursery and school, moving house, learning to read, coping with his mother's return to work. The arrival of a new brother or sister is just one of many other potential life events which demand adaptation.

Don't feel guilty

Ridiculous though it may sound to the intellectual part of ourselves, it is easy to feel guilty at landing a baby on our unsuspecting first child!

Penny, who followed up three-year-old William with Davina, says,

> I used to look at William, playing so happily in the sandpit, and think, poor little thing! He's no idea what's going to happen. Tears would come to my eyes! Now when I see them playing, I think how ridiculous I was. I was partly worried about how he would react, but if I'm honest I must say some of those feelings were really about me. I would feel very weepy at the thought of the big change ahead, and how it might affect my relationship with William.

It has been said that by having another baby, you are effectively telling your first child he isn't enough for you. However, this needn't be the whole story. Your own attitude will certainly influence the message your toddler gets, so why not alter the focus of this by side-stepping the negative? It can be turned around: the family is being expanded. If you say that more is coming into everyone's life, you leave out the question of insufficiency altogether, together with its devastating hint of broken expectations.

Toddlers will quickly pick up on any tincture of guilt and doubt in you, though it would be impossible to banish all such feelings from yourself! Anyone embarking on a second pregnancy has taken on a massive responsibility – another human being's life – and, as we saw in Chapter 1, some wavering reactions are to be expected. However, be quite firm about telling yourself that you're not doing your toddler any favours by feeling sorry for him; sentimentality of this kind will only weaken his security. What you can do is reassure him as to your love. Spend extra time reading to him; set aside a couple of half-hours each day which is his time, with no distractions or interruptions; take him to toddler swimming classes (nice for you when you get heavy, too) make the most of your time together before someone else arrives to share the fun!

Meeting other children

If your toddler hasn't had many children his own age in his life so far, early pregnancy is a good time to start expanding his circle. He needs to build up his own 'outside life' so he has other resources to fall back on as your pregnancy advances. More contact with other children tends to happen naturally in any case once children hit the two-and-a-half- to three-years mark and become more independent and sociable.

So, explore local playgroups, mother-and-toddler groups and day nurseries. Contact your local authority for details about workshops and day classes with crèches. Local authorities also run those invaluable one o'clock clubs, which are free apart from nominal sums for cups of tea and coffee. Obviously, the facilities and people vary, but they can be good places for both you and your toddler to make new friends. Look at the noticeboard in your local library for other activities – and while you're there, ask if the junior library has a regular story reading time which your child might attend.

If you already have friends with children around your toddler's age, they could prove worth their weight in gold with just a little initiative from you. For example, you could organize regular meetings into an informal playgroup, giving other mothers and yourself time off, and the children a chance to see their special friends.

Other friends

Your toddler's other friends don't all have to be children his own age, of course. Now could be a good time to start forging closer links with gran, or with the friendly neighbour down the road – anyone who wants to become that bit more special to your child. A pet is also a consideration – but only of course if *you're* prepared to do all the work! A puppy who needs a lot of walking and training is not a good idea as pregnancy progresses and your fatigue level rises; a low-profile rabbit might be more of a possibility.

Now could also be a good time for your child to start a new activity such as swimming or a dance class. Check out your partner's availability on a Saturday morning!

Introducing babies

The earlier months of pregnancy can be used for introducing the subject of babies in general. Again, friends can help naturally with new babies of their own. Or perhaps you've noticed someone in your street who's just had a baby – a good opportunity for both her and you to gain a new friend. Another idea is to keep an eye open for babies in parks, supermarkets, crèches and one o'clock clubs. Of course, you don't have to make the whole of your life together one long baby-hunt, otherwise your child will become first suspicious, then defensive! In fact, he's more likely to bore you with the subject – most children are fascinated by these creatures who are so much smaller than themselves.

While looking at babies, you can give information and lay down a few ground rules at the same time. For example, you can point out that tiny babies are fragile, that they must be picked up with care, that they're not like dolls, and so on. You can also explain how they tend to cry when they're unhappy, that they spend a lot of time asleep, and that they need to be fed at the breast or with a bottle. At some point later in your pregnancy you can make all these points more real by borrowing a baby for an afternoon. A very young one will help your toddler understand that tiny babies aren't yet able to play, although an older baby will make him aware that, after a bit, they can be enjoyable companions. Can you borrow *two* babies?

Another point to talk about to your toddler is his own babyhood – so near in time, so far off in development. Perhaps because of the enormous changes children go through in the first few years of their life, many seem to have a need to consolidate at around three years old. They become fascinated by their own babyhood and play at regressing – calling themselves babies, pretending to cry, and so on. This of course often coincides with the arrival of the new baby, but it can happen anyway! Try making a special photo album of your first child's development, with snapshots arranged in chronological order, especially for him to brood over. If it all gets too much, don't try and argue him out of it – just agree quietly that for now he is a baby, and try and change the subject!

What to tell . . .

Young children are acutely sensitive to what is going on around them. Lowered voices won't keep a secret. If you want to test this, whisper something controversial about your elder child to your partner ('Lucy's got pink hair'); the chances are that your toddler will swing round and deny it vehemently!

How much to tell does of course depend on the age of your toddler. Someone poised between his first and second birthday won't understand too well what you are talking about. Between two and three years the idea will become clearer but of course your toddler won't realize the implications of the birth, or that there will be someone else around all the time. To some extent, your maternal judgement will guide you as to what your child will understand, but even so, it can be difficult to know how much even an older child really takes in.

Don't worry about details ('and the Daddy sperm met the mummy egg down the little canal', etc) unless your child is desperate to know, just get the general idea across. Avoid overkill. Let your child take in what he can, on his own terms; he has many weeks and months ahead in which to assimilate the rest.

It's also easy to become confused about exactly what you are telling your child. Are you keeping the information biological? Are you focusing on life changes after the birth? Are you predicting what his feelings will be? Keep to plain information for now, and make it short and simple: a baby is on the way, it's in Mummy's tummy and will come out later, your child will soon have a new brother or sister.

Preparation of your toddler can only go so far. It is important to realize that (just like you) your toddler may enjoy the *idea* of a new

20

baby without fully realizing what the reality entails! No one can live the future. However much he begs you to get him a baby sister or brother from the shops, a real baby will always have that element of true-life surprise.

. . . and when

This is a difficult question. A child's grasp of time remains uncertain even up to five years old, and at around two to three, 'tomorrow' is still an ungrasped concept. At first, however, you only need to introduce the idea of the baby in general, without as yet going into details of time and place.

There's probably no real need to tell your toddler anything until your shape has changed, say, between five and seven months. You might want to say something before this however to stop graceless visitors popping out the truth before you can stop them. 'Are you looking forwards to having a baby brother or sister?' is a question designed to spring mistrust of the human race on a child!

Later on, perhaps two or three weeks before your due date, you will need to warn your toddler more definitely that you'll be going into hospital. You'll need to make sure he understands the arrangements that have been made for his care – staying with Gran or having a friend come over. He also needs to know that he can visit you, and that you'll be home very soon. Perhaps on one hospital visit you could both pop your heads round the door of the post-natal ward, so he has an idea of what to expect when he comes to see you.

As the growing baby becomes more real to you, you can share this with your child. You can feel the movements together; you can ask him what name he would like for his new sibling; he can help you choose any items needed at the shops; he can put his ear to your tummy to hear if the new baby is 'talking' to him – anything which develops his own special share in what is going on.

Ante-natal visits – taking your toddler

Even if you are lucky enough for your hospital to have a crèche, there is no guaranteeing your toddler will agree to stay with a strange lady flourishing a bunny rabbit at him. One way around this is, if possible, to go with another pregnant friend who has a first

21

child whom your child knows well, and see if they will both go into the crèche together.

Ante-natal visits can be a special time together, another chance to share your second pregnancy with your child. From a child's point of view, the routine examinations provide many new things to look at – the doctor, who may kindly play the baby's heartbeat on the fetal monitoring system especially for the toddler to hear, or the midwives pressing their trumpets to your tummy. Even the waiting can provide points of interest: other pregnant women, other children, people coming and going, weighing machines or passing trolleys, babies, and so on. Of course the interest may well run out before you are actually seen, but to some extent going to the hospital can become an acceptable outing for your child.

Don't forget to treat ante-natal visits as you would any other excursion – stocking up with snacks, drinks and books for your child as well as for yourself; damp flannels for wiping sticky mitts and mouth; nappies if still needed; the toddler's cuddly or special toy; change of clothes; and anything else to prevent boredom. Obviously, it isn't a good idea to take your toddler if you're exhausted or unwell. In late pregnancy especially, it might be better to arrange visits during his nursery hours, or to leave him with family or friends.

Pregnancy and birth games

Your toddler can assimilate what's going on through play. With just a little help from you, you can encourage him to have his 'own baby' – either one bought especially for the approaching event, or an adaptation of an existing toy. Soft rabbits, toy soldiers and rag dolls can all be babies – you may be surprised at what your child adopts!

Sitting down deliberately to play these games may seem a little self-conscious, but it is worth trying to give your toddler all the help you can, even if he's very young. At some level, it all goes in! If you don't prepare properly, you may end up with a confused child who doesn't respond well to the birth. So, some suggestions for games:

Ante-natal class rope in some dolls and teddies, add a tape measure with which to check tummies, scales for weight, paper and pen for a co-operation card, and perhaps a cheap doctor's kit (from Woolworths or similar).

Hospital visit organize some dolls in improvised beds, add some babies made from bundles of cloth or smaller dolls, and let your toddler play at visiting mothers with babies in hospital. You can refine further on the game with another doll for the nurse, miniature bunches of flowers, etc.

Baby care invest in a small 'disappearing milk' bottle (milk vanishes when it's upturned, magically re-appears again when stood upright) with which to feed the 'baby', find the old baby bath, baby towels, talc and even a tiny nappy or two. Toyshops stock doll versions of these but your toddler may prefer the real thing. Let your toddler play at being the baby, too.

New baby books

There are many books you can read to your toddler to prepare him for the advent of a sibling – so long as you don't expect the books to do all the work! Some books focus on the mechanics of pregnancy and after the birth; others concentrate on feelings of jealousy, which might be better left until the feelings actually emerge. Have one or two ready, just in case.

Don't forget to introduce plenty of other new subjects too. Let babies and birth be just one of the topics you cover during this period, when your child's growing awareness of the world make a variety of books welcome. Now could be a good time to join your local children's library if you haven't already done so. Here are some books you might find helpful:

Rosie Runs Away, Maryann Macdonald and Melissa Sweet, Heinemann.
A delightful look at the feelings of toddlers experiencing the realities of life with a baby.

The New Baby, Anne Civardi and Stephen Cartwright, Usbourne.
Gives a plain and simple overview of Mum going to hospital and new baby arriving.

Baby, Geraldine Taylor, Ladybird.
A general look at the nature of babies and family life with a new and growing baby.

A New Baby in My House, Ruth McCarthy and Helen Averley, Julia MacRae, Random Century Group.
Contrasts the life of a baby and her elder sister, with emphasis on the latter's power and privileges!

101 Things to do with a Baby, Jan Ormerod, Viking Kestrel.
A gentle hint to slightly older children (3–5) that babies can be fun to play with within a family context.

Alpaca, Rosemary Billam and Vanessa Julian-Ottie, Fontana.
Contains the comforting moral that no matter what new distractions come along, old friends (the rabbit, Alpaca) will always be wanted and loved.

Ben's Baby, Michael Foreman, Beaver Books, Arrow Books Limited.
Traces the coming of a baby from the point of view of a small boy – it's seen as a natural event, like the seasons, which gives joy to all.

Spot's Baby Sister, Eric Hill, Heinemann.
For a very young child, a simple and positive approach to the arrival of a sibling.

A present 'from' the baby?

It's lovely to consider the implications of giving when a new baby is in the vicinity. The baby itself can be viewed as a gift to the whole family.

If something of this attitude can filter through to your child, the question of a present to him can be part of an event in which giving is not calculated in terms of financial or emotional costs. There is however a certain stern moral attitude which dictates discouragement of a 'sweetener' for the toddler on the grounds that it can foster envy and insecurity. This may be so if the toddler is given a present because of parental guilt, or as a vague attempt to make something up to him. But a present is traditionally an effective way of saying hello from a new being, and it needn't be one way.

The toddler can also choose something from the shops for the baby, or be given the chance to donate something he has used and enjoyed – a mobile perhaps, or a small teddy. It doesn't have to be something suitable, just something he wants to give.

If your toddler hasn't already adopted a baby from his existing

24

toys, he often finds a doll now for the practical reason that small children will copy the adults around them. If you are going to spend time with a baby swathed in your arms, then your toddler needs to have the materials to copy you. Many parents now are not as shy as before about giving boys dolls too. But it is possible to get away from the baby theme and simply give the toddler something he really wants. Ideally, this should be something which will keep him happily absorbed for a while – not something which demands minute, constant attendance from you! To get this right, buy as late as possible, to avoid giving him something too complicated, or, alternatively, something which he will have outgrown by the time the birth comes round.

3

Practical Considerations

It probably isn't that long since you and your first bulge did that mammoth tour of all the great baby shop names, trundling from one department store to the next, wondering if that tingling sensation meant an incipient faint or even the start of labour, and trying to decide on just how many muslin squares would be appropriate. All this when you weren't even sure what a muslin square was really for (making home-made cheese?) Well, now you know! But, having the time and money to wander round the shops in search of the perfect babygro are probably luxuries consigned to the past. This time round, your luxury may well be *not* having to go to the shops, at all, except for some newborn-size nappies.

Because you have enough equipment and things to spare from your first baby, the practicalities of preparing for a second baby can easily be pushed to the back of the mind. Of course, you'll cast an eye round the house for a corner for the cot, and no doubt you can rejoice in one working pushchair. Also, there are all those carrier bags of outgrown clothes in the attic, just waiting for the right moment to be sorted through.

But when is the right moment? It can be surprisingly elusive in a second pregnancy. Perhaps like many pregnant women you don't want to tempt fate by starting preparations too soon – but before you know it, the busy toddler-filled days have rolled by and you're three weeks off your due date, heavy and exhausted. Not the best state for starting your preparations.

Again, if you're pregnant relatively soon after having a first baby, you may find yourself procrastinating because it all seems to have come round so quickly again! Maybe you're not sure if you have the energy to face it yet. This can be especially true if you're feeling at all ambivalent about the second pregnancy, and perhaps wondering if you were wise to plunge in again quite so soon. Deferring preparations can be a way of not thinking about the forthcoming birth.

This isn't at all to say that second-time mothers-to-be simply fish out a handful of first-size vests from the appropriate bag and call it a day. Naturally, most mothers want to make some gesture of welcome towards the new baby, however small, to buy a new outfit, or a clean cuddly, or a tiny silver bracelet – a personal gift of welcome that hasn't been used by the first child.

However, this isn't the same as trying to think through the daily nitty-gritty of having another baby around. Nor is it really a case of equipment. It's more matters such as where the baby will sleep, how mobile you'll be with two children, and whether there are any little extras that would make your life easier second time round.

Although these matters may seem trivial, being clear about them in your mind – or not – can actually have quite far-reaching repercussions. A muddled attitude towards how the new baby will fit in to your life is more likely to engender confusion after the birth – a way of wasting energy that will be urgently needed for other matters. Mothers who assume the second baby can just be 'fitted in' are creating stress for themselves in advance, because the baby won't have a proper place in the house. Of course, new babies do take time to grow into a family, but forethought can make this process smoother.

For example, Laura had no settled place for baby Alicia to sleep – one night it was the computer room, another the sitting room or even the landing. As a result, she was always harried at night and would carry her sleeping baby to what seemed the best spot with her heart in her mouth lest she awaken her. This attitude seemed to persist into the day, too – she was always telling Alicia that she was a second baby and would just have to put up with waiting for feeds and attention! Although this was lightly and lovingly said, there was a grain of truth in it, and Laura herself didn't feel completely comfortable about the way Alicia fitted in with the rest of the family. In the event, she moved to a larger house where Alicia and her brother Henry could have a room each, and things became easier at once.

Even in cramped surroundings, however, it is possible to ensure the new arrival has a special corner of his own. Of course, it isn't always possible to arrange every last detail in advance, and your plans may not work out after the birth, but if you do need to make adjustments then, at least you have a structure within which to work.

Practical preparations are also a vital part of the emotional ones: no doubt you remember from your first pregnancy carefully making some little item that wasn't really needed, or going into the nursery for the hundredth time to see if there was anything else to do . . .

Have the house ready

Are there any jobs which have been lying around waiting for the perfect moment? If so, now's the time to make the decision – either that they must be done, and soon; or, that you're not going to waste energy thinking about them any more.

Part of second-time motherhood is accepting the fact that the house will become more rundown, and chaotic. Even if being houseproud is one of your priorities, you run the risk of becoming exhausted after a few months if you try to care for two children, manage other activities, have some sort of social life, and keep up a pristine house as well. So you might as well start accepting the inevitable now, unless you have a will of iron and energy to match. Before deciding, bear in mind that all tasks are more difficult when you're pregnant, never mind with a demanding toddler around. Ask yourself whether going ahead with, say, repainting the hall, is going to be unbearably frustrating with your little one trying to dip her fingers into the paint and desperate to help all the time. And talking of help, exactly who will be doing the work? How much can you expect your partner to do?

So, first divide tasks into large, smaller, and routine. Large tasks are those which involve major reconstruction work, like moving the bathroom or putting in a new kitchen. Are they necessary? Do you really want them? Can you face the upheaval and the probable delays while you're pregnant? And will the final advantages outweigh the disadvantages of building in progress? Will your toddler get in the way? Will the jobs seriously disrupt her routine?

Second, the smaller tasks: fixing a door that's wonky on its hinges, varnishing a floor, or painting a room. Again, are they needed or do you just feel you ought to do them? Details amiss can be very niggling even if they don't interrupt daily life too much. So one idea is to lay aside a Saturday for a blitz on all the little jobs.

When it comes to routine tasks, think about which parts of your housework you can most easily let go, both during pregnancy when you're tired, and when you have a new baby to care for. Make a list if it helps: what are your priorities? Does it really matter if you dust the skirtingboards once a month instead of once a week? Will anyone know or care if you don't hoover under the rugs for a while? Also see which jobs you can delegate. Can you find a window-cleaner or someone to do the ironing?

PRACTICAL CONSIDERATIONS

Something that is worth considering with a second baby is creating extra storage space. This can be drawers under the bed (save them from discarded chests of drawers or wardrobes); an extra trunk or two; a wicker laundry basket, or even tea chests (remove the nails). Shelves are an especially worthwhile investment of time and energy, as they do help you get organized: shelves for extra toys, books and jigsaws, for nappies and clothes. Don't forget that as your toddler gets bigger she will have more toys, and you won't be throwing any out to make room because the younger child will need them.

Where will the baby sleep?

This very much depends on your individual circumstances, and on your personality. If you have a large house, you may well want to give the baby a bedroom of his own, and if you or your partner can find the energy to redecorate it, you really are in the luxury class!

The memory of the first few weeks with a new baby may well have lost its edge, so do bear in mind that the second baby will probably be in with you to begin with – or at least well within earshot. Wherever you decide, try and stick to your decision, and decorate the corner so that everyone in the house knows this is the baby's special place. This will help your toddler get used to the idea of another person taking up space, too.

Should the baby and toddler share a room? Some parents put them in together from the start simply because there is nowhere else. If your toddler is a light sleeper, however, and you don't want the baby in with you, you may want to find another spot for the baby – a corner of the living room, for example. There's also the consideration of leaving the baby alone with the toddler. Even if your toddler means well, her climbing in to the baby's cot is a move fraught with danger, especially if you are asleep in the next room and don't hear. One older child decided to cut the baby's hair one quiet Sunday morning – the whole family ended up in casualty with a baby and a bleeding ear! On the other hand, if the children share a room from the very beginning, the toddler is more likely to feel she has a real share in the baby, and you can always slip in to collect him for feeds.

Certainly, once the baby is able to fend for himself a bit more, sharing a room can be nice for both children, especially if one tends

29

to get frightened at night. It can also be a way of keeping them happy in the early hours of the morning when you don't want to get up but when they do want company!

Do you need extra clothes/equipment?

Even if your second baby is to be born at a different time of year to the first, babygros and nightgowns are fairly standard wear for newborns and can be made warmer by adding cardigans and shawls. However, if your first was born in June and your second in November, or vice-versa, you might like to lay in a couple of extra outfits for extremes of temperature.

It's also as well to be prepared for a change of size. Second babies are usually bigger than first ones, so do prepare all your age 3–6 month garments as well as the newborn size, which your baby may either not fit or grow out of very quickly. There's also the reverse possibility of the baby being smaller. For example, if you had a large boy the first time, you may just follow it up with a petite girl.

This brings us on to different clothes for different sexes. If antenatal tests or your mother-in-law's infallible second sight have revealed that your baby is a different sex to the first, you may not be able to resist splashing out on a few suitable outfits. Otherwise, you'll just have to wait and see! Mostly, it seems that people don't mind putting girls in blue babygros, but they do object to putting boys in pink ones – macho stereotyping still rules OK! True, it is tiresome to keep explaining to all the nice old ladies in the street that he is in fact a boy when they all lean over the pram cooing, 'Isn't she sweet!' Before you do start spending, though, do go through those old boxes of clothes – you may still have some forgotten pristine gifts of all colours from the first time round. It's up to you – and your budget. Generally, though, people don't give as many presents to second babies as to first ones, so don't rely on gifts so much.

It's also a curious fact that the first baby's clothes may not actually suit the second baby, even if they are the same sex. After all, babies have different looks, different shapes, and different personalities.

One extra piece of equipment which some second-time mothers are quite shameless about using is a dummy, another example of the way second-time motherhood can erode your ideals! Of course, this doesn't have to be so: but it might be worth considering for times of possible stress.

Likewise, many second-time mothers don't mind allowing the baby a bottle, and may introduce it from day one, even if they are breastfeeding for the majority of the time. Research has shown that second-time mothers are more relaxed about feeding their babies in general, and are more likely to feed on demand. It may also be comforting to know that breastfeeding itself is often much easier the second time round. Nevertheless, having been tied by breastfeeding to one baby, some mothers want their baby to take an occasional bottle so the baby can more easily be left with someone else.

Then there may be other items which you just didn't get round to trying the first time, but which you feel might make a difference this time; a sheep fleece for the baby to lie on, for example, or a baby listener for a larger house. Some mothers give terry nappies another try, especially if they bought them first time round and hardly used them, though there's no doubt disposables make life with two children far easier. With the growth of environmental awareness, nappy options may have changed since your first baby; for example, it's now possible to buy wool instead of plastic pants (see Addresses).

Do you need a double buggy?

Moving from a single to a double buggy can bring a return of pram nerves to the most seasoned mothers. Remember the first time you ever took your first baby for a walk? How the traffic swerved too near and you couldn't get the pram up or down the pavements? A double buggy seems like that: too wide, too cumbersome; and too expensive. New buggies are costly, although you can sometimes get good deals second-hand.

However, it may be money well spent for the sheer mobility it will give you, especially if you don't have the use of a car during the day. If you want to visit friends who live just that bit further than the toddler can walk, or go to a different park, a double buggy can be invaluable. Once you get used to the width and the weight, it isn't that much more unwieldy than a single buggy, and it is possible to take it into bigger stores when you go shopping. Another real bonus about the double buggy is that, if you're stuck with two whingey children who refuse to take a nap, and you're desperate for an hour's break, you can pop them both in and wheel them down the road. With any luck they'll both be asleep by the time you get to the end!

One idea is to wait until the baby can sit up and then buy a light double stroller. Meanwhile, you can take the new baby in a sling – which many mothers prefer anyway because it feels safer – and have the toddler walk or go in the single pushchair. Of course it partly depends on the age of your toddler – a hefty three-and-a-half-year-old probably won't need a pushchair often enough to make the purchase of a double buggy worthwhile, as opposed to the more easily tired two-year-old.

Involving the toddler in preparation

Letting your first child share the preparations can be an important part of helping her adjust herself to the idea of the new baby. Letting her help makes it a project in which she has a part, not some mysterious activity which is monopolized by you! Perhaps the toddler can help move her own clothes out of a drawer to make room for the new baby's; line the drawer (and her own) with special scented paper; help fold away the first-size vests and babygros.

She can also help prepare the baby's corner, wherever that is to be, make up the cot (probably try it out, too), hang up mobiles, and so on. She can go through her toys with you to see if there are any which she no longer plays with, which can be relegated to a baby bag. Now too might be the time to ask her if she wants to pick out anything of her own to give the baby, or to buy anything at the shops. She can also accompany you if you need to buy any bits, and will probably appreciate a share of the cotton wool, baby lotion and newborn nappies for her games. (Do keep any sample bottles for her, too.)

Your future lifestyle: do you want a change?

The classic pregnancy is one in which some upheaval, some turmoil, is going on – moving house, starting major household repairs, or simply redecorating. You might think such situations would either be arranged in advance, or strenuously avoided so as not to add to the stress of pregnancy, but the opposite seems to be true. Perhaps pregnant women need some outer change to make manifest in material, visible terms the immense changes going on within!

At any rate, a second pregnancy is just as likely as a first to provoke thoughts of change, but do consider whether such changes are really vital, or whether they can be postponed until after the birth. To take an extreme example, Samantha, who had been working in New York as a full-time publisher, had decided to return to England when she became pregnant again unexpectedly. She arrived with husband John, an American writer, and four-year-old Elizabeth, when she was six months pregnant, with nowhere to stay but her family! Their generosity did help, and Elizabeth knew England from a long visit the previous summer, but, says Samantha, 'I wouldn't do it again!' Even moving house within this country, traumatic at the best of times, needs careful planning and some luck.

On the other hand, early pregnancy *is* a good time to re-assess your life. A second baby marks you 'family' with a more definite stamp than a first. At this point some couples do decide on lifestyle changes; some move house in search of a bigger garden or better local facilities; others leave the town for the country. And, you will almost certainly need to think about work again (see Chapter 12 for more on this.) Whatever you decide, do bear in mind that the changes don't *have* to be implemented during your pregnancy – life does continue afterwards!

Nearer the birth: other practicalities

A second birth means an intensification of the preparations you made first time round: all the extra shopping and cooking for the days after the birth when you wouldn't be able to get out as much. Or does it? Is it really worth loading yourself down with extra bags of flour and tins of tomatoes when you're heavy with pregnancy and have another child to manage? Do you then come home and exhaust yourself further by knocking up a few meals to freeze and keeping your toddler from climbing onto the stove at the same time?

You can of course shop while she's at nursery, or give your partner the shopping list. Or, you could just forget about all those nourishing casseroles you were so diligent about first time round. If you don't have someone to help you cook after the birth, why not forget your conscience for a while and go for the frozen pizzas and fish pies, the ready-made chicken stews, to tide you over the first couple of weeks. If you choose wisely (watch the salt content for your first child's sake) they can be quite nourishing, and you can always make them more so with an extra sprinkling of grated cheese and/or wheatgerm, plus some raw vegetables and fruit. They are of course more expensive, but in the scheme of things it won't be long before you are marshalling your own vegetarian lasagne together once again. Don't forget that some convenience foods are good for you, too – baked beans, tinned tomatoes, frozen vegetables, fish fingers and tinned fish, for example.

It is an idea to lay in something extra for yourself to eat after the birth. Because many second-time mothers leave the hospital earlier than the first time, they're at home when that post-labour hunger hits them – and then, it's all too easy to slip out to the corner shop for a big chocolate bar! So, lay in some private gapfillers – figs, dates and nuts; frozen home-made bread pudding; biscuits made with oats, wholewheat flour, wheatgerm; cheese; a tin or two of tomato soup or oysters or guavas – whatever you think will help!

4

Your Toddler's Routine

With two small children to look after, it definitely helps if the elder
one is as settled as possible in every aspect of his life – eating,
sleeping, and general behaviour. By far the most important of these
for most mothers is sleeping, which is why nearly half of this chapter
is devoted to the subject. The last thing you want is to have to get up
in the night not just for a crying baby, but also for a crying toddler.

A well-established general routine, with meals around the same
times, and a set bedtime, also gives your toddler more security. It's
worth noting that many children, especially if poor sleepers or
excitable, can benefit from a calmer, more regular life. Overstimu-
lation can leave some children bored, unsettled and liable to cry
easily; they may also develop a habit of constantly calling for their
mothers because they are so used to activity being provided for
them. What with outings, nursery, dance and swimming classes,
and more, it's easy for a child to be always on the go. Sometimes he
needs nothing but a quiet space in which to unwind and slide into
some private creative activity of his own, whether that's pretending
to be a dragon or just daydreaming. Regular reading sessions with
your child, and a quiet time after lunch, can also help calm a child
who has a tendency to become overtired, as does that age old
remedy, fresh air and exercise. A young child, who is learning all
the time, and has plenty of outside stimulus, does need the stable,
familiar environment which you can provide.

If you can, aim to accomplish any big changes either in early
pregnancy or well after the birth. This sounds neat enough, but the
most likely of the changes is your first child's starting playschool or
nursery; or you may be moving house, starting building work, or
trying to find a childminder – none of which may occur at the desired
time! However, these will be easier for your toddler to swallow if
the other areas of his life are relatively stress-free. If on the other
hand you're fighting over mealtimes or bedtimes, the bigger events
will cause more upheaval than they need. Even if the baby has
arrived, and life is muddled, you can still aim to make your toddler's
routine run more smoothly.

One good idea is to institute a really regular nap if you haven't already done so. If your toddler falls asleep at different times each day, now could be the time to encourage a sleep for example after lunch so you can rest while pregnant. Maybe after the birth you can persuade the baby to sleep then, too.

Are there any other areas where, without pushing your toddler, a little encouragement will help him to do things alone? For example, a small stool in the bathroom may help him climb into the bath, on to the toilet and up to the sink without you having to lift him. Or, for the same reason, you can ask him to walk from the front door to the car, or up the stairs. He can tidy away his toys at the end of the day – make a game of it. If you've always rushed in to the rescue when your toddler attempts something tricky, stand back for a minute and see if he can manage alone. After all, the time is coming – or is here – when he will have to make do with less of your attention in any case.

Eating

The picky eater materializes anywhere between the first and third birthday: a typical breakfast for a two-year-old might be half a slice of toast. During pregnancy you'll probably be more aware of what you're eating, and so notice pickiness more. Obviously, it's best not to force the issue: the vast majority of healthy children eat when they are hungry. Just make sure your child drinks plenty and has access to fresh fruit; and, if you are worried, keep a food diary for a few days and then take it to the doctor.

If you're keeping an eye on your nutrition during pregnancy, now could be a good time to experiment with different recipes together. A new interest in food from you might rekindle a difficult toddler's enjoyment of food, especially if you let him help you with preparation.

Sometimes you might want to look behind the food problem to see if there are any other emotional factors involved, the most obvious being the approaching birth. Eating problems can turn into a power struggle between mother and toddler and, like other things, this can persist after the birth, complicating relations with the new baby. It's certainly a worry you can do without during pregnancy, as Susan found out:

Three-year old Tina was extremely picky. This dated from the beginning of Susan's pregnancy when Susan had been ill with a threatened miscarriage. Happily this had passed off, but Tina would still eat only the same few foods – chicken, potato and bananas. Susan couldn't resist slipping her biscuits between meals; Tina's father, Rick, also nagged her about her eating. As the time approached for Susan to give birth, Tina's general behaviour deteriorated so much that they went to see the family doctor, who felt that Tina was under too much pressure. Susan was advised to leave Tina alone at mealtimes and to be quite firm about not giving her anything in between. Once Susan made up her mind, the problem was resolved quite quickly and the whole family settled down to await the birth.

Toilet training

People always speak of 'two in nappies' with a shudder of horror, as if this were the last word in inconvenience, muddle and frustration for a mother. However, it needn't be that bad. By now you must be experienced enough in nappy changing to realize that it takes little longer to effect two nappy changes than one. Carrying two sets of nappies back from the shops is of course heavy work, but if you order in bulk, nappies can be delivered by major stores such as Mothercare, Boots and branches of John Lewis.

However, it does help to get most of the toilet training over with before the new baby arrives, if only because you will have more attention to give your toddler. Also, when your toddler sees the new baby using nappies, he may be keener to hang on to his own! Bear in mind that it does depend on your child's age. Most children just aren't ready before 18–20 months – often later – and may not shed the night nappy before three years.

Being pregnant (or with a new baby in tow) you'll want to spend as little time as possible on your hands and knees clearing up accidents, so it might be better to wait until you can see that your toddler is really ready to be trained before trying.

This is how Penny managed it with William.

I waited until he could tell me he wanted to do a wee before he actually did it. Then we just went straight into overkill! I cancelled our outings for a week, stocked up on juice and sweets, took his bottom half off, and kept the potty near us all the time.

Every time William used the potty, he got a sweet. Luckily it was summer so we were outdoors, but it was a very boring week! On the other hand, I was seven months pregnant and didn't want to leave it any longer – and it did work, give or take a few accidents afterwards.

Dressing

An independent dresser certainly helps in late pregnancy when you can hardly bend down to do your own shoes up, and again later when you're busy with the new baby. With an older toddler, however, this is often a case of can but won't. Or of can up to a point, but then gets fuddled with back-to-front trousers, dresses worn over jumpers, and socks added to tights. You may find that if you lay the clothes out in the required order your child can manage them; or, he might be able to manage the bottom half but not the top half. Let him do what he can; he will appreciate the trust you show in him and may one day surprise you by dressing alone completely. He might like to choose his clothes for the day – and, later, the baby's (you can hide away anything that's vastly unsuitable). You can also train him to put garments away in the appropriate drawers, to put his dirty clothes in the laundry basket, and to hang up his coat and hat on 'his' peg when he comes in.

From cot to bed?

Moving your child into a bed is a good idea because you will need the cot for the baby at some point, and won't want the toddler to think he's been thrown out to make room! With this in mind, you might consider folding up the cot and putting it away for a few months, perhaps painting it a different colour, so that your toddler doesn't immediately remember it as 'his'. Of course, the new baby won't actually need a cot for the first three months (or longer) and can go into a Moses basket or cradle.

Some people launch into bunk beds as soon as they know another baby is on the way, which can be great fun for the toddler, providing a good climbing frame with space to play on top, as well as an area below which can be made into a house with the help of blankets. If you do want to buy bunk beds, check that you can sit up reasonably comfortably on the bottom one or you may face a few years of bedtime reading bent almost double!

If you're going to leave the change until after the baby's birth, do allow a few months to elapse before you move your toddler.

Pre-school care

Owing to the vagaries of nursery school waiting lists, it isn't always possible for your toddler to start when you'd like. The ideal time is probably a few months before the birth so you are on hand to give the required support without the baby and post-natal fatigue. Starting sooner rather than later will also give you much-needed resting time in late pregnancy, as well as valuable space after the birth for babycare, work, shopping, tidying, or just catching up on more rest.

If you have a choice of school or playgroup, and aren't sure which to choose, go for one which is near to your house rather than one which is further away. When it comes to the crunch, convenience does outweigh cosmetic advantages such as newer paint on the slides or a better-looking hamster in the cage. Of course, you shouldn't settle for something you dislike just because it's near, but getting a baby *and* a toddler ready to go to playgroup takes long enough without a 30-minute walk as well.

If your child has to wait a long time for a place, it might be worth considering a local childminder; the local social services will provide a list, or the playgroup grapevine, or the doctor's noticeboard. Your child then has a place to go to which is his, which isn't dependent on his family, and which can provide reassurance and support in times of change. Most childminders take a few children, so that your child will be able to make friends of his own before the baby arrives.

Sleeping problems

This is the one area which is vital to get right well before the birth! Training one child to sleep can, frankly, be a nightmare, so who wants a double dose with two in the house? Unfortunately, some toddlers respond to change with lots of night waking, making it difficult for you to respond without feeling cruel and insensitive. After all, in a few months' time, your toddler will have to share you.

However, for the sake of the whole family, it is probably better to be firm unless you are fundamentally very relaxed and can cope with endless night disruptions. Like everything else, it depends on your personality and needs. However, most pregnant or nursing mothers usually respond rather poorly to two or three night-wakings!

It may also be the case that night wakings have been happening anyway, irrespective of the approaching birth, and that your toddler has never developed a pattern of sleeping through the night without disturbance. In this case, it usually isn't any good waiting for the birth to happen in the vague hope that your elder child will 'settle down'. He might, but what's more likely to happen is that you will just end up full of resentment towards him for waking you up when you also have the baby to deal with.

> Mary, six months pregnant, would get up two to four times a night to deal with Johnnie, who had the habit of waking up and crying for no apparent reason until she came to soothe him. Mary's mother warned her she was 'Making a rod for her own back', but Mary, though exhausted by day, couldn't bear leaving Johnnie to screech for nights on end until he got the message, and there *were* nights when he slept through without disturbance. The problem was amplified after the birth of baby Rose, when Mary had to get up for two callers – and they woke each other up as they were in the same room. Finally, Mary put the baby downstairs in the living room and was able to convince Johnnie that night wakings were no longer appropriate, which she did mainly by dint of sheer repetition, and praise and small rewards when Johnnie didn't disturb anyone. It did take quite a long time this way – about two months – but Mary felt it was preferable to leaving him to cry.

Not all pregnant women would have such stamina! It's also easier to train a younger toddler who is still in a cot – once he's in a bed you have the added work of taking him back every time he gets up. Yet another good reason for dealing with a sleep problem before the birth is that you will have more confidence when it comes to handling the younger child. Sleep problems tend to run in families; you don't want to increase or even cause a problem in the younger child by uncertain handling, though it's also worth noting that second babies tend to sleep better than first ones, probably because parents *are* more confident with them.

What can you do?

Much advice on sleep problems involves parents in a heroic struggle to endure the sound of their child's screams in the middle of the night, plus the remarks of neighbours the next day! It's even more difficult when the sound of your toddler's crying wakes the baby up – the nearest thing to hell for a second-time mother must be two small children howling at 3 am. One obvious answer is to move the baby out of earshot, but in a small or open-plan house this isn't always possible. In this case, however, try taking the baby into bed with you for a few nights while you and/or your partner train the toddler. This is something which many second-time mothers are more willing to do than the first time round anyway, just to get a good night's sleep. You can always train the baby later, and, as toddlers often sleep more heavily than their younger siblings, the baby's crying may not wake the toddler as much as you think. You could also try taking the toddler into your bed for a few nights if you feel he's insecure. This may be especially true after the birth if he comes in to your room in the early morning and sees you giving the baby a feed in bed. He doesn't know the baby hasn't been there all night! However, this is only likely to work if the sleep problem is a temporary one – if it's been going on for some time independently of the birth, you may simply be creating a new habit. You can try putting the two children in to the same room in the hope that they will calm each other down – but don't bank on it. Research has shown that sharing a room makes little difference to real sleep problems.

Below are summarized a few recommended ways of persuading a toddler to sleep better, which can also be used for an older baby. How old? Some medical advice advocates leaving it until after the first year, other authorities say you can start at six months. Generally, the younger the baby, the more likely it is that you'll have to repeat the training at some point, as it tends not to 'stick' until the child has passed his first year.

Before starting to tackle the problem, it is vital to *make up your mind* that you are entitled to remain warm and comfortable in your bed at night. Doubt will sabotage your attempts quicker than anything else. As a pregnant woman, newly-delivered mother, or seasoned mother of two, you need all the sleep you can get, especially if you are breastfeeding and/or do other work during the day. It is possible to survive broken nights for a few months, of course, but eventually you risk burning out and your health can suffer.

It's true that getting your child to sleep can involve crying, and you may feel that allowing him to wake up the baby is more than you can bear, but it's also true that it will eventually end in tears for everyone unless you and your partner get the sleep you need. Your relationship with each other, the way you treat both children, and your general efficiency and well-being, even your health, can all be damaged. You need sleep for your growing baby's sake while you're pregnant, and to maintain your ability as a caretaker after the birth.

If you still secretly can't believe all this, and feel your toddler's needs overcome yours, remember, you have all day in which to convince him of your love and to sort out any aspect of life with the new baby which might be bothering him. Also, you can always adapt any of the following to suit your own situation – there's no merit in inflexibility if your child's screaming is just going to reduce you to a nervous wreck.

What's more important is that you are convinced you are doing the right thing. This conviction will enable you to keep a clearer head and release your natural maternal intuition which can otherwise become blocked by uncertainty and resentment. This will in turn enable you to work with your child in a structured but flexible way which can balance everyone's needs.

If you can't face the struggle, just take your child into bed with you – why not? Children shared their parents' beds for centuries before modern society ordained separate sleeping, and sharing is still the norm in some parts of the world. It's unlikely to be for ever, and you can always move the child back to his own bed later, when you feel strong again.

If you do go ahead with sleep training, you will probably need your partner's help. Another solution can in fact be to have your partner go away – some women feel stronger alone, though this might be best left until well after the birth, when you're likely to feel stronger too.

Hilda had been trying on and off for a year to get both Henry and Alicia to sleep through, as she was frequently disturbed by them both. Her husband Matthew undertook to train the baby, but his efforts were ruined when the baby soon afterwards became ill.

Henry would also wake up and come into their bed and finally Matthew just went to sleep in the spare room. Hilda felt he needed his sleep as his job was very demanding. It wasn't until he went away on a week's course that she realized it would be much easier to toughen up without Matthew around to worry about as well. She took her courage in her hands, put the children to sleep at opposite ends of the house, and just let them scream, going in to check on them every 20 minutes. 'If they woke each other up crying, it was just too bad!', she said. 'I felt here was a golden opportunity I couldn't afford to miss.' This was so successful that Matthew came home to a different wife, greatly refreshed and beaming after a couple of good nights' sleep!

Helping your child sleep: the methods

Do remember that the following suggestions are only starting points. Adapt them and build on them as you feel appropriate, every family is different.

First, some things to try:

1. A general chat. Is something bothering him? Is he apprehensive about the approaching birth? Could he be feeling guilty because he doesn't like the new baby? Is he having nightmares? Keep your ears open for any hints he may drop during the day, and follow them up then and there; otherwise, perhaps the best time for this is during the bedtime routine when you're both snuggled up with a book and he's relaxed but not too sleepy.
2. A regular, calming night routine in which he spends some time with you alone, without the baby.
3. Practicalities like a pre-bedtime snack, a potty left by the bed, extra warmth in the room, and a night light.
4. Also try moving your child out of a cot into a bed, or onto a mattress on the floor if he's very young – some children hate being 'caged in'.

(A) *The so-called extinction method:* brutally clear – just leave them to cry for three or four nights. Most problems are supposed to clear up within a week with this method.

(B) *The so-called controlled crying approach:* going in at regular intervals (5–20 minutes) to assure the child of your presence, making him comfortable if necessary with nappy change, drink, etc,

43

and leaving quickly again, without chat or cuddles. Again, this is supposed to get results within a week.

(C) *Staying:* you stay with your wakeful child but interact as little as possible. In this way he knows you are around but that you are not available for any more than reassurance. You can soften this one with tucking up, patting, cuddles and verbal reassurance, too.

(D) *Withdrawing:* if you want to proceed further in a gentle way, aim at settling him with progressively less contact. For example, if you normally sit on the bed, sit by it; then move your chair further and further towards the door until you finally get outside. Give brief verbal reassurance; avoid long talks or much eye contact. You could pretend to sleep yourself, or read a book.

(E) *The alarm clock trick:* the child isn't allowed to get up until an alarm clock or buzzer goes off. You may have to take your child back to bed the first few times before he cottons on to the idea; works better with older children (three-and-a-half upwards).

(F) *The reward system:* can be used in conjunction with an alarm. Stickers for a chart, a cheap bag of toy animals given one by one, sweets – whatever works – can be given to the child in the morning who has not woken up during the night.

If all else fails, ask for professional help from your doctor or health visitor. Some surgeries now provide sleep counselling clinics, and just talking about the problem can help.

5

Reactions from Your Partner and Others

When you announce your second pregnancy, you can guarantee that on the whole there will be a lot less fuss than the first time round. People seem to expect you to take a second pregnancy in your stride; after all, you opted to become pregnant again with your eyes open, fully aware (presumably) of what you were doing; and, you lack the interest of novelty. To some extent you will share this general diminution of anxious care about yourself, this rather bracing, more grown up approach. What Mrs Jones down the road insinuated about the size of your bump (surely *not* twins?) will swiftly fade away under the influence of your toddler, who has decided to teach her small plastic animals to swim in the toilet, or who suddenly becomes agitated about something invisible and unnameable beneath the stairs. It is a comfort to know that as a busy mother you're much less likely than the first time to be at the mercy either of your own feelings or of other people's comments.

However, you can still be liable to all the increased sensitivity that accompanies this special time. A careless comment can still reduce you – a hardened mother with perhaps more than a year's total pregnancy behind her – to tears. There will be days when no one quite understands how you feel, days when your partner gives you the wrong kind of look before leaving for work, when your mother-in-law is too busy telling you how not to spoil your first-born to listen to how you're feeling after another desperate tantrum. But, you will have less time to think about it all.

Your relationship with your partner will change again, as it did during the first pregnancy: and will change more after the birth. The myth that children 'cement' a marriage needs careful examination. In fact, one of the two highest stress points in a marriage is when the children are under five (and in their teens). Marital psychotherapists even have a recognized term for the discontent that can fall upon a married couple when children come along – the U-turn of marriage. Satisfaction with the marriage declines, and doesn't increase again until the children grow up and leave home.

This sounds like a rather drastic warning to anyone considering having one child, let alone two, but it is misleading to attend to statements and statistics with the kind of expectations that are formed before having children. Perhaps it would be more true to say that after the event, couples form a new kind of partnership in order to cope with the demands of bringing up a young family – a partnership in which their own needs and satisfactions fall a natural second.

This partnership takes a new turn with the birth of a second baby. To many, it really turns them into parents, rather than a couple with a baby. It makes parenthood that much less voluntary; partly because, on a practical level, it becomes that much harder to arrange breaks from care-taking – people who don't mind baby-sitting for one may feel a little daunted by two. You may both feel slightly dismayed at the way life is grinding you into roles – Mother and Father instead of individual partners, and couples can find themselves thrown on their mutual resources more than before. With the decline of the extended family and increasing social isolation caused by geographical factors and growing urbanization, many couples are forced into being much more to each other – support system, friend, confidant, babysitter, source of inspiration, fellow washer-upper, and more.

Whereas before it was possible for one partner to take the child while the other went out or went upstairs to relax, both sets of hands are often vital with two children. Their demands are so immediate, and so ruthless, as to leave little time or energy for considering the finer points of any other relationship. When you've spent a full morning at the doctor's surgery with a sick toddler, and an even fuller afternoon with a baby who wants to be amused, you reach the evening not really caring that your partner has forgotten Valentine's Day again. All that matters is that he's come home from work; he's there.

Some of your best friends during this period will probably be other mothers, especially other pregnant mothers. With any luck, you'll have a good batch of them left over from your first set of ante-natal classes or your first stay in hospital. They're the ones most likely to empathize when you feel weepy or grumpy, to realize how expertly your toddler can play on your stretched nerves or how beastly you feel for being too tired to take her to the park that afternoon. They're the ones who come round a day or so after the birth full of delightfully practical help – camomile cream for sore nipples and big packs of nappies for presents, as well as lots of attention and a small gift for your toddler! Make the most of them!

The pregnancy: your partner's reaction

Do you remember your first pregnancy test? When he got up with you at the chill crack of dawn and hovered about, too excited even to have a cup of tea until the test had showed positive? Well, this time, don't be disappointed if he stays in bed! Likewise, when you first feel that magical flutter which indicates new life kicking inside the womb, you may neither of you feel inclined to spend long minutes with his hand poised on your tummy, waiting with bated breath to see if it happens again. He knows, as you do, that it most probably will. Just as your own reactions to the second pregnancy are likely to be different, so are those of your partner. And a common reaction is not to appear as excited as the first time. As has been said before, in many ways this is *your* pregnancy.

Of course, most men are just as delighted as the first time that they're to be a father again; it would be wrong to deny that thrill which comes at the thought of an unknown life coming to join the family. But it is quite common for this fundamental reaction to be swiftly overlaid by the cares of the world – money, responsibility, loss of freedom. Whereas one child was a joyous adventure into the unknown, two can easily represent a burden to care for. Now that you both know exactly what having a child involves, the news of a second pregnancy is likely to be greeted with far more gravitas than before. And, joking reactions such as 'Help! What have we got ourselves into?' may have more than a grain of truth in them!

After the initial reaction, many men go on to show far less emotion than before at the news, though their behaviour can speak volumes. Some throw their energies into their jobs, becoming near workaholics at the prospect of having to support an increased family:

Laura's husband, David, an accountant, responded to the news of a second baby with a bunch of flowers and a prompt disappearance! Suddenly, he had to stay late at work every night, and sometimes went in on Saturdays too. It wasn't until Laura was three months pregnant that David told her he had hated his work for the past two years now. He hadn't wanted to say so previously for fear of unsettling his new family, and was only forced to now because Laura, fed up of battling with her toddler Henry, pregnancy sickness and exhaustion alone, had tackled him forthrightly about his family responsibilities. After a long talk, it was agreed that David would speak to his boss about how he was feeling and if necessary look for another job. In the event, he was able to change offices and drop part of the work which had been causing dissatisfaction, and this made him happy enough to stay.

Another reaction can be a subtle kind of distancing which takes place because the man feels threatened or even excluded by the mother-and-baby bond. Even in this age of the so-called 'new man', research has shown over and over again that in the majority of cases it is the woman who takes on the extra responsibility for the children; and that men don't do as much as they might to help with childcare or around the house even if they are emotionally supportive. It is easy, and common, for a man to feel shut out by one baby and mother – and this is of course accentuated by the prospect of a second. In practice, however, the second baby often means that the man becomes more involved than before – through sheer necessity. However, in reality, most of the responsibility for organizing the practicalities of family life still tends to be taken by the woman:

Hilda's husband, Matthew, a head of department at a local school, was pleased at the news of his wife's pregnancy, but she found it hard to get him to help as much as she wanted, especially when she was tired from looking after their two-year-old Toby. The first time round, Matthew had been very solicitous, making her rest and worrying over every little twinge she felt – this time, he seemed to expect business as usual, saying only, 'I leave it to you to take care of yourself in a sensible way'.

Also, he didn't seem to want to talk about the new baby much, seemed a bit bored by it all, and went out more alone when as often happened Hilda was too tired to accompany him.

To some extent this changed after the birth of Ben, when Matthew would take Toby out a lot more. Hilda still felt she had to do far more than him, however, and that Matthew wasn't really interested in the new baby. Then, when Ben was around ten months old, and more mobile, vocal, and generally out to charm, Matthew suddenly seemed to 'come to', in the words of Hilda. He played with the baby more and was quite happy to take care of him while Hilda went out. From then on, Hilda felt the family was united once again, after around an 18-month gap.

Hilda's story illustrates an important point – that it can take time for a family to settle down again after the addition of another person. As Hilda puts it:

One day you wake up and suddenly realize you're quite happy to be living with this person again, that you do have things to talk about and you do enjoy a cuddle together. But before that, there's a long stretch where you both feel you're doing too much and the other person isn't doing enough. It's a bit like when you first get married and have to adjust to each other after the honeymoon period. It's more complicated to shake down again after the second baby because there are now four personalities in the house.

Other reactions can take unexpected forms, too. Some men become what you might call 'world rights bores', earnestly concerned about every issue which crops up in the news, highly opinionated and authoritative on national and international politics, and as worried about the state of the economy as if they were the chancellor of the exchequer. What happened to the man who once whisked you off for a surprise weekend in Venice? Has he become a permanent casualty of two-pronged fatherhood? Happily, this state of affairs is often temporary, as Sue and Rick found out – though it doesn't feel like it at the time:

After the birth of their second baby, Angela, Susan and Rick shared a subdued kind of post-natal depression for about a year. Says Susan: 'Everything seemed to go very grey. Rick was always going on about all the terrible things that were going on in different parts of the world, and although he said he could remain emotionally detached from them, I couldn't! It brought me down very much, which in turn depressed him. Looking back, I see we reacted to the birth by taking our new responsibility overseriously, and, of course, we were often very tired. Also, we didn't have much money. We were rather isolated, too – we'd moved and anyway we didn't really have the energy to go out. In the end, what turned the corner for us was going away for a holiday at Christmas – although we couldn't really afford it, that fortnight helped us to start enjoying family life again'.

The arrival of a second child can usher in a phase which tests you and your partner to the limit. Of course, life does settle down again – and it may do so more quickly if you can summon the energy to put a little effort into it. Obviously, if you do feel that you and your partner are losing touch a little, it's important to talk and be honest about your feelings; but try and have some constructive suggestions ready to put into practice, too:

- Go out more: try and aim at a regular slot once a week so you know you will have time together. If you are shattered by evening, try booking a babysitter for Saturday lunchtime and go out then.
- Have at least one regular family outing at weekends so your partner doesn't become excluded, even if it's only a trip to the local park to let your toddler loose on the swings.
- Take an extra holiday or long weekend: for example, hiring a cottage in the UK is easy with a toddler (aim for no more than a two-hour journey) and can provide you with a few inexpensive days' break to recharge the family's batteries.
- Institute breakfast in bed: with tea, biscuits, books, magazines (and mess, but don't worry about it!) Let your toddler join you.
- Get a babysitter: twice a week to take over the hardest part of the day between 5–7 pm, when everyone's tired and the children have to be bathed, given tea and put to bed. While next door's teenage daughter is fending off the splashes upstairs, you and your partner can be swanning around with drinks downstairs.
- If you can afford it, get more paid help for the jobs you dislike, such as ironing or hoovering so you can conserve some energy for human relations.

Your partner's changing relationship with the first child

A second pregnancy and birth traditionally provide a time when the father and the first child grow closer to one another. Ideally, you doze off on the sofa, indulging in visions of kite-flying and football in the park, or dance classes and puppet theatre at what passes for the local art centre. The reality may be a harassed man with one cold, muddy child; or an early return home because Punch and Judy proved just too terrifying. Never mind. In many ways, first children and fathers do form special bonds at this point.

It isn't all due to the fact that you are suddenly less available. Your first child is older now, more articulate, capable of a wider range of activities. She may still fall asleep in the car when an eager father takes her swimming, but on the whole she is probably at an age where a mutually satisfying dialogue can be maintained.

Taking the child out does seem to be a paternal speciality, and, while no right-minded mother would really carp at this, it's a common complaint that fathers take all the fun jobs, and wriggle out of the routine ones such as bathing, changing and feeding. Perhaps the best way to tackle this is to have a formal timetable of duties which has been worked out to your mutual satisfaction. Research has demonstrated that in many cases, women just don't talk about their dissatisfaction with men and the amount of help they need, so maybe activities do need to be deliberately worked out, not just left to chance.

It can feel very difficult to break through a status quo in which you may feel over-burdened with childcare, especially if your partner feels he already does quite a good share. The best thing to do is to replace this with a new status quo, in which it soon becomes taken for granted that Saturday mornings are 'mum's time off,' or Wednesdays 'her going-out night'! Introduce one change at a time, keep it small to start with, and make it regular.

Communicating the toddler's needs

It is all too easy, if the major responsibility for your first child has been yours, to regale your partner with endless details about what she likes, what she does when, what she eats, and what activities she's capable of. 'Oh no, she only ever has cereal for breakfast', is

51

guaranteed to put a damper on a man who's happily feeding his daughter a healthy mix of apple and cheese. Children *are* creatures of habit – but if your partner can create some new ones, why not?

In fact this can be very useful. Susan's husband, Rick, forgot to put a nappy on Tina one night when he put her to bed. Susan didn't discover this until the morning, when she also found that Tina was still dry! From then on, in spite of three or four accidents, Tina never wore a nappy again. So, use your second pregnancy to let go some of your responsibility for your first child. After all, it won't be too long before that responsibility transfers to others anyway, first at nursery, and then at school.

What others say: another baby already?

Other people's attitude to a second baby can be distinctly un-settling. No sooner does your toddler hit her first birthday than they start murmuring questions about whether you are going to give her a brother or sister to play with. Then, when you do go ahead, the keenest type of interest likely to be manifested is a kind of shock that you're pregnant again, so soon! Some souls may even hint that such a speedy second pregnancy is a shade indecent. After this, the interest typically wanes – in stark contrast to the first time when the same people were busy telling you to put your feet up.

This doesn't apply to true friends, of course, who can win your gratitude by taking your toddler off your hands every once in a while so that you and your growing baby can relax. There's nothing like a second birth for sorting out the sheep from the goats!

However, it is good advice to hang on to everyone you were remotely friendly with before, because as a second-time mother you do risk becoming more isolated. It can be more difficult to go out with two children, especially if their routines are very different or if you have a practical block, such as no car. Public transport, hard-going with one child, can make for very discouraging experiences with two – though of course you have to weigh this up against the stimulus of whatever is awaiting you at the end of your journey. Certainly, people who live near you, or who will visit you, become worth their weight in gold, even if they're not precisely the ones you might have chosen!

However, you probably observed the way some of your friend-ships changed after your first baby. You no longer had much in common with some people; others, you felt closer to than before. Again, this is a process which intensifies after the birth of a second baby. Although getting out and seeing people is even more necessary with two than with one, there isn't that much spare energy to waste on people whose wavelength is very different to yours. With two children to look after, anything that involves a lot of strenuous effort to keep up is bound to fall by the wayside. Do try and keep up with old friends, though – a postcard or quick phone call will do. In time, your hands will become more free, and you may find yourself very ready for the company you were too exhausted for just a few months previously.

6

Your Hospital Stay: Introducing the Baby

It is vital to get it right when it comes to your hospital stay, mainly for your first child's sake, but also for your own physical and mental comfort. In the busy toddler-dominated days, it's easy almost to overlook the fact that you'll be going through another birth, but even if your main energy is directed towards looking after others, you must spare a thought for yourself!

The first point to be clear about is that your toddler is unlikely to suffer from a few days' carefully planned separation from you – and you will need those days, to rest after the birth and to get to know your new baby before plunging into family life again. A few days is of course the ideal. Not everyone can arrange for the older child to be looked after for that long, but, unless you are very strong, one or two nights away is a must – four or five even better!

Explaining to your toddler

Final preparations of your toddler can be complicated by the fact that you don't really know when you are going into hospital, and don't want to say too much too soon in case your toddler becomes worried and unsettled. Explain clearly to your toddler what will happen two weeks or so before your due date, even if you've mentioned it before. He still won't really know when you are going but, on balance, it is better that he is a little unsettled by the idea in advance, than that he's completely taken by surprise when you depart. There is always the possibility that you will be early!

It's a mistake to try and foretell exactly how long you'll be away – your plan of a two-night stay might extend into a week because of unforeseen complications, and in any case, a younger child (around two years) won't be able to grasp the time schedule. An older child (three-and-a-half to four) may have more of an idea but is still unlikely to be able to reckon the days exactly. You also put pressure on yourself to be back by the stated time and may already feel the tension which stems from this – tension which can communicate itself to your toddler.

Try and exude a relaxed approach to the fact that you'll be away. You can try and explain your absence in terms of his routine. For example, 'Tonight Daddy's going to put you to bed, and read you your story, and tomorrow when you get up in the morning, Daddy will give you your breakfast and take you to nursery. Then Granny will pick you up . . .' and so on. Be quite detailed, so that he won't be looking for your familiar face at the usual times and places – or so that the idea of someone else caring for him is at least introduced.

Smoothing his way

There are practical things that can be done near the birth to prepare your toddler for the upheaval in his routine. Arranging a practice run of your birth arrangements will make the hospital separation less of a big change for him. So, if he is going to stay with a granny or an aunt, send him away for a trial night a few weeks before your due date so that he has a taste of other people's cooking, other people's routines. Or, go away yourself if your toddler is staying home (but not too far if you're past 36 weeks!).

If the toddler is going to stay at home, it is worth stocking up with his favourite foods. Obviously, you don't want Granny to pander to him by arranging the spaghetti alphabet to spell his name on his toast every mealtime, but familiar foods will be a comfort to him while his routine is upset. Similarly, if he has any food fads, now is not the time to be correcting them. Make sure whoever is caring for your child is aware of any strong dislikes.

If your toddler has pet names for anything important, you could note them down on a piece of paper, along with any other instructions you want to give to your principal caretaker – bedtimes, toilet details, meal times, and so on. Nap-time is an important one to mention if your toddler becomes impossible when he's tired – knowing the right time is only fair on your caretaker! You could also make a copy of your list to keep in a safe place (Laura's husband David promptly lost the original list!). In any case, your toddler has to learn to communicate with other people in times of need, and most small children are fairly adept at making their desires felt.

Another idea to help palliate your absence is to leave postcards or letters from you to be given to the toddler every day, especially if you know you're going to be in hospital for a few days, perhaps after a planned Caesarean. Children love receiving mail anyway, and will feel more in touch with you, even if they're to visit later the same day. Again, this depends on the co-operation of whoever is looking after your child.

You could also make a tape of yourself reading your toddler's favourite stories, or of yourself just talking with your toddler. Aim to do this a week or so before you go, and listen to it with your toddler before you go, so that it becomes a familiar link. Finally, one really good way of giving your toddler a lift during your absence would be to throw a party for him and his friends – if your caretaker can bear it!

> Susan's mother was a gem. As soon as Susan had gone to hospital in labour, she rang four of her friends to ask if their children could make an impromptu party the next day. The children, who were all around three, were quite happy to mill around together, being too young for any organized party games, and when Tina went into hospital to see Susan and baby Angela, she was full of the party. To Susan's question of: 'What did you have to eat?' the prompt reply was 'sausages and chips'. Evidently happiness could reach no higher!

All in all, this can be an exciting time for your toddler – the only problem will be re-adjusting to the comparatively slow pace of life once you're back home!

Goodbye!

Saying goodbye to your toddler is always recommended – when you drop him at playgroup or at a party – so that he understands you're an honest, trustworthy person, not someone who will sneak off the minute his back is turned! The same applies when you are leaving for the hospital. It's also important because it really *is* goodbye – goodbye to the life he has known up until now, and this needs to be acknowledged, though not dwelt upon. For the same reason, saying goodbye can be important for your sake: you too are leaving behind an exclusive mother-and-child relationship.

If he's asleep when you leave, should you wake him up to say goodbye? Some people do recommend it – and you may have to wake him anyway if you are going to take him to someone else's house. On the other hand, if you think you will be able to arrange a brief visit fairly early the next day, it might be better to leave him snoozing, especially if he usually grumbles when woken up. You could however whisper goodbye – who knows, it may go in on some level, and at least you can then trustfully tell him you did say it!

Arranging help

Briefly, the more, the better! Now is not the time for scruples, or for fear of imposing on people. Sometimes you have to impose; and, if necessary, to ask for help. Sometimes people are, with typical British tact, too delicate to ask for fear of intruding or because you seem so competent! Be quite firm about accepting even half-hearted offers, and state clearly what help would be most accept-able. Do you want someone to do a shop for you while you're in hospital? To take your toddler to the park one afternoon? To babysit for you during your final ante-natal appointment? And, there are two occasions on which help is really indispensable: when you go into hospital for the birth, and for a few days after you come home.

Because the baby might be early or late, arranging help for your time in hospital can be tricky unless you have a willing mother or similar – someone who doesn't mind coming to stay a week or so before your due date and just hanging around until it all happens. Almost as good is an obliging relative or friend who lives 5–10 minutes away and is ready to be woken up in the middle of the night should labour begin.

Some people book a maternity nurse or other paid help for the weeks immediately following the birth, and perhaps for a week before the estimated delivery date, too. If you can afford it, this might be a godsend, but you do need to be careful about who you choose. Bear in mind that, as the mother of one child, you will probably have a much stronger idea than before about how you want to handle your second baby – and a maternity nurse may have equally firm ideas of her own. On the other hand, she will spare you having to get up in the middle of the night, even if you still have to half-wake for a breastfeed!

You could also spend the money on extra domestic help, or on someone to look after your toddler more for a while. Contact a local nanny agency for best results; advertisements invariably bring a swarm of the wrong kind of people which is exhausting and hardly worth it for temporary help. Alternatively, if you don't have much money a trainee nanny could be·a help, though again the standard varies enormously from individual to individual. To find one, contact your local library for a list of colleges which train nannies.

Help when you come home is one of the key factors to a good start to life with two children. Of course the first few days aren't going to make or mar relations between yourself, the toddler and the baby, but it feels like it at the time! In any case, it is easy to over-estimate how much you can do after a birth, especially with two children.

Remember, your toddler has no idea of the massive physical upheaval you've just been through and is more than likely to be his usual demanding self, grouchy because you've been away, unsettled by all the attention he's had from Gran, scrambling onto your knee with a book every time you breastfeed, and rolling around in the Moses basket the minute it's vacated (sometimes even before!). Ideally, then, there should be someone in the house waiting to welcome you when you come home – not the helpful friend who says she'll be down tomorrow as soon as she's finished her shopping, although she too has her place!

Failing all this, or if arrangements break down unexpectedly, you may have to fall back on your partner as the sole source of help. This may mean going through at least part of labour alone while your partner looks after the toddler. This is hard, but it's as well to be prepared just in case. Because you don't know when labour will start, taking time off work after the birth can also be problematic for your partner and may depend on the sympathy of his boss. If the worst comes to the worst, he will just have to take a couple of days off sick, because if you have no one else, you will need him! Without adequate help, you may not be able to manage, and your toddler may suffer as well as you.

Laura came home the day after her second birth, on a Thursday afternoon, and was alone all Friday – her husband David felt he had to go back to work as it was very busy, and she assured him she could manage. She deeply regretted this by midmorning because she found herself so irritable with her toddler, Henry. He continually got on her nerves by climbing over everything, including her, and Laura ended up shouting at him a lot. It certainly wasn't the ideal introduction to his little sister Alicia she'd planned, and there were tears all round before David returned that evening.

Preparing for the birth – your comfort

Now – what about you? You're probably so used by now to being a mother and putting your toddler's needs first that you may have almost forgotten you are going to be giving birth before long. What with ferrying him to and from nursery, coping with his manic/depressive swings of mood, and clearing up the ever-renewed mess, there may not be that much time to prepare yourself. However, it is important, even though you've given birth before. You do have needs of your own, even if being a mother normally gives you little time to consider them.

So, consider those needs. Bearing in mind your first labour, can you spend a few minutes each day visualizing how you'd like your labour to go? Have you re-considered the possibilities when it comes to pain relief? Is there anything you feel you'd like to take into hospital this time?

If you can afford to, it's an idea to line up some little treats for yourself when you come home – a new nightdress, some bath salts, an absorbing book. With two to be responsible for, your own needs will be even more pushed to the background, and there will be times when a 20-minute soak in a scented bath can make all the difference to your day.

First meeting with the baby

That important first meeting between the toddler and baby is most likely to take place in hospital when your child comes visiting, unless you have arranged for your child to be away for a few days after the birth. Certainly, it is a good idea to arrange at least one visit, so he has the chance to see the baby in the neutral hospital environment before it comes home. Also, your toddler will be reassured by knowing exactly where you are. You'll need to draw on all your stage-managing talents when it comes to formally introducing the baby to the toddler – a deceptive casualness together with a perfect sense of timing! However, if you consider most formal introductions, how much idea do they really give of the people involved? Usually it isn't until a few meetings have taken place that reactions can really be appraised, or that different personalities show themselves. Likewise, a glimpse of a crumpled, sleeping face, or hearing an indignant hungry wall, aren't going to give your toddler any true idea of what life with a new baby is really like.

So, try not to regard this as The Meeting which will set your toddler's reaction to his sibling for life. In a sense, he won't actually be meeting the baby until much later when the baby is more responsive, able to smile, to sit up and coo, to wave arms about and, later still, to play.

Having said this, don't be *too* casual – make sure the toddler sees the baby and understands the reality of what has happened as much as possible. It can be quite easy to balk the introduction if you're a little nervous or unsure!

Mary wasn't quite sure how to tell her two-year-old that she would be away for a few days. She had talked a lot about the baby that was on the way, and assumed that Johnnie had a good idea of what was going on. In the event, she went into hospital two days before the birth in order to be monitored and finally induced, and Johnnie visited her in the ante-natal ward. This meant of course that the first two times he came in, there was no baby. Then, because the post-natal ward was so noisy, Mary was desperate to come home as soon as possible. The result was that the first time Johnnie saw the baby was when Mary was taking her home. 'We didn't really know how to manage it,' recalls Mary. 'The doctor had just discharged me and I picked up the baby and said, "Look, Johnnie – here's Baby," then we left.'

This bare introduction made for an unhappy start for Johnnie. Suddenly, the reality of the baby hit him, and he burst into screams which continued all the way through hospital corridors to the exit. Mary, carrying the baby and still weak from the birth, could do nothing; and Johnnie lay on the floor and refused to be carried by Mary's husband George, who became furious! 'Later of course I realized Johnnie should have had time to assimilate his first sight of the baby', says Mary.

It is hard to think this straight after a birth when you've been woken all night by other people's babies, and disturbed all day by other people's visitors. However, you can help by making the visit as much of a treat as possible. There's no need to introduce the baby at once – simply greet your toddler as you would after any separation, giving him a special cuddle and kiss. Have some little gift ready to distract him with, such as a packet of tiny animals or some crayons –pack it in your hospital bag in advance, and let your toddler unpack them himself. Or ask your partner to buy you something (check out the hospital shop if you're stuck.) Or maybe he could arrive in time to share a hospital meal with you – anything to soften the introduction!

Hilda's experience of toddler-visiting was much happier. She'd had an easy birth and was feeling well and quite happy to lie back and let the nurses do as much work for her as they wanted! Toby came in just in time to share her supper ice-cream, which he was favourably impressed by, and she'd had the forethought to pack two of his favourite books in her bag. Properly coached in advance, her husband Matthew also did his best to make the visit enjoyable for Toby by giving him lots of attention and taking him off to visit the rest of the ward. When finally introduced to the baby, Toby was enthusiastic, seeing her as a continuation of all the fun he'd been having! Toby did want his mother and the baby to come home at once, but registered no more than a token protest when the visit ended and he had to go home.

When it comes to actually introducing the baby, take it easy and play it by ear. Your toddler may well come round to the subject of the baby himself. If not (it's easy not to spot a tiny sleeping baby) point her out as casually as you can: 'Have you seen the baby over there?' Do give your child time to absorb this new being at his own pace and don't force a reaction or ask him what he thinks if he appears blank to start with.

A likely reaction is wanting to touch and hold the baby. Allow this, but mount a careful if unobtrusive guard, even a gentle toddler may not know his own strength. The easiest way for him to hold the baby is for you all to sit on the bed with the baby draped across your laps, while you, mum, support the head.

If you're feeling very washed out or have had a lot of stitches, or if you're wired up to a drip, you may not want your toddler to visit. In this case, it's only sensible to wait until you feel better. As stated before, it won't hurt your toddler to be away from you for an extra day or two, and, although a hospital visit will pave the way, it doesn't really matter where he first sees the baby – in hospital or at home – so long as you manage it with reasonable tact. (See the next chapter for more on initial reactions and the early days.)

Coming home

Unless you're sure you feel up to it, it is probably best not to rush straight home in order to be with your toddler. In contrast to the first time round, many second-time mothers love every minute of their time in hospital, appreciating the fact that nurses are around at least part of the time to help, and that meals are brought to them. Some even positively enjoy the hospital food! 'Lovely stodgy meals which remind me of schooldays', was the verdict of both Laura and Penny. Penny adds, 'I was completely selfish about staying in – I decided that the rest of them would just have to manage as they could, and I stayed the full five days. Although I had an easy labour, I knew the first few weeks when back at home would be tough, so I was determined to have a rest while I could'. Penny was lucky in that her kindly mother-in-law ran the fort during her absence; but, as mentioned before, take advantage of any half-willing help!

Choose your time to come home carefully. Of course, it isn't always up to you to decide on the hour when you can come back, but try and make it at a time when your toddler won't be tired or hungry. Sounds like common sense? Again, it's easy to forget in the post-birth atmosphere.

Susan, for example, was discharged around 7 pm after the doctor was delayed by an emergency Caesarian. When Rick came to collect her, he also brought a very tired, grumpy toddler who was well past her bedtime by the time they got home! Although Tina had enjoyed her first visit to the hospital, by now the novelty had worn off and she was bewildered by the break in her routine. She had spent two days with her aunt and uncle, and, in the words of Rick, they had 'spoiled Tina rotten'. To make matter worse, Rick left the special present from the baby in the boot of the car – a point that wasn't at all appreciated by Tina. It did go some way to calming her down on the unpleasant drive home, but Susan then had to spend her first few hours at home soothing Tina and putting her to bed with lots of extra cuddles and stories when all she wanted to do was go to bed herself. Luckily, the baby slept through it all!

Home birth

The medical profession seems marginally more willing to allow home births to women who have had healthy, normal deliveries first time round, and it certainly eliminates many of the worries about what to do with your toddler. In addition, he can share more fully in the birth, and will be able to see the new baby sooner – all in all, he'll be far less excluded. Obviously, you'll still need someone to look after him during the birth itself, though there's no reason why he shouldn't be there part of the time if you're not in too much discomfort. Incidentally, a few women have their toddlers in with them for a hospital birth, too – at least part of the time. If this appeals, you can always ask your hospital if they would mind letting your child stay.

7

Initial Reactions and the Early Days

At last, the time has come for the new baby to join the family. The long waiting of pregnancy and the hard work of birth are over, even if you can still feel your stitches! It's lovely to be back in the comfort of your own home, and normal life is within view once more. With any luck, you're being brought nourishing little meals and cups of tea by someone kind, and being urged to build up your strength.

Perhaps you're afraid you'll need it! Because the time has now come for toddler to live with baby, and to come face to face with the reality of a sibling. It's the end of her exclusive relationship with you: from now on, there are two to share your attention; two to dress, two to undress and bathe; two to qualify for cuddles, lullabies, and outings.

How your toddler manages the change depends partly on how you've prepared her, but in the last issue, her reaction can't be predicted. It's easier on everyone if you don't have any expectations about how your toddler will behave. Try not to make even any silent demands that the toddler love the new baby, or be grateful to you for providing a companion. In fact, these feelings may well manifest themselves, either immediately or in the future, but you can't conjure them.

The first six weeks after any birth are hard, whether or not you have an older child to deal with. Your body is working overtime to get back to normal; all the high hormonal levels of pregnancy have suddenly dropped, leaving you prone to weepiness and depression; your blood volume, which increased by 30 per cent during pregnancy, has also dropped, which means you tire very easily. Breastfeeding may also be using up your energy, and of course, there are all the emotional re-adjustments which need to be made, not forgetting the notorious post-partum blues on day four or five.

After your first birth, maybe you felt nostalgic about your pre-baby life. Now you may have the same feelings when you consider your first years with your toddler – so special because she was your first child. Don't worry if you feel like having a good weep over her old baby photos – you'll soon be rejoicing in new pictures of both children. These feelings do pass. However you feel, it's important to conserve your energy while the baby is still tiny and sleepy. Even if you do feel well, delegate whatever you can and don't undertake unnecessary tasks. This time, you need to think long term – when your baby 'wakes up' from that initial doziness, you will be far more aware of having two children!

It can be easy to sail through the first few weeks, when your newborn is relatively undemanding and perhaps there's help around, and then become exhausted because you've taken too much on. Keep as much strength as you can for the inevitable eventualities of parenting – such as both the baby and the toddler getting bad colds in two or three months' time. Even without extra disturbances, you need time to adjust to your new responsibilities, both physically and emotionally. So, rest as much as possible while you can, even if the initial period is easier than you anticipated.

It may of course go the other way around – a hard start initially, followed by an easier time once everyone's settled down. The first six weeks after the birth are often dreaded by second-time mothers because they do dimly recall how demanding they were from the first time round! You don't yet know the baby, he's an unpredictable entity who hasn't yet settled into a routine; breastfeeding may not yet be completely established; you may be suffering post-natal complications such as mastitis or infected stitches.

There's also the possibility of having a difficult second baby after an easy first one, as some women discover. If you didn't experience evening colic, disconsolate crying, or refusal to feed the first time, they can be very upsetting second time round. Parental confidence can be given a definite blow! However, to be positive, second babies *are* traditionally much easier than first ones, and it's more likely that you'll be pleasantly surprised at how soon the baby slots into family life, even if the first weeks are hard going.

Handling the first few days

A good general rule is to be as relaxed as you can – remember, your toddler doesn't have to be jealous. Another piece of advice is to leave the baby be as much as possible – after all, you haven't been home for a few days. Even a day's absence is a long time by your toddler's standards, and she needs a while in which to adjust. Some toddlers are distinctly grumpy with their mothers after even an afternoon's separation; crying when picked up from the child-minder is a classic example, even if they've been perfectly happy all day. So, your toddler may need to work this out of her system before she is really ready to take in anything new.

If possible, arrange to have the baby asleep or taken out of the way by your partner or a friend when toddler and baby first share room space at home. When you first arrive home, once you've given your toddler a greeting cuddle, it might be nice to settle down to a book together, or to a quiet meal – something undemanding and sedentary in view of your probable post-natal sensations! Ask her what she's been doing ('Nothing' is a fairly typical answer!) and follow it up with some general chat about the details of life: whether she can still put on her own cardigan, whether she gave the cat his lunch, or whatever. Sometimes a tactful partner has in his turn stage-managed a welcome, with a little card designed by the toddler, flowers and perhaps a gift for the baby. He can go on to be a tower of strength for your first child, distracting her with lots of attention for those inevitable times when the baby needs attention, and reassuring her generally as to parental love.

Other people can help your toddler adjust to the baby over the first few days. Visiting midwives, who are of course highly experienced in this area, can be especially helpful. Some behave as if they had all day to spare, giving the toddler a cuddle, chatting to her, and showing her all the mysterious instruments she carries in her bag. If yours is one of these, make her a big cup of tea and be grateful!

What you don't want is the over-eager visitor who dashes in exclaiming, 'Where's the baby?' while you see your first child's face fall.

Penny had always been on friendly terms with the woman up the road, who often babysat for William and was a particular friend of his. In a tactless moment, she rushed in demanding to see baby Davina, whom she then cooed over for some minutes. William went very silent! Fortunately, the visitor recollected herself and then gave William the little gift she had brought for him, telling him how lucky he was to have such a lovely baby sister.

In fact, most people have a pretty good idea of how not to tread on your toddler's sensitive feelings. Visiting aunts and uncles, and good friends, playschool leaders and nursery teachers, can all play their part in helping your toddler adjust to the new arrival.

Your expectations of the toddler

This is mentioned because it is suddenly easy to expect too much of your toddler, forgetting how very recently *she* was your baby. In comparison with the new baby, she may seem so much bigger and so much more able to fend for herself. However, a walking, talking child does not necessarily mean a rational human being – though she may in fact empathize to a surprising extent.

Susan for example was struck by Tina's reaction when she brought baby Angela home. Over the first few days as they all settled down together, she said, 'Tina seemed to be concerned at how much I had to go through – constant breastfeeding, trying to soothe a crying baby, being tired. She always seemed to know when I had been awake a long time at night, and would ask me about it in the morning. What made it a bit pathetic was that she would invariably follow it up with, "But I'm being a good girl, aren't I, Mummy?" ' In the end Susan had to explain to her sensitive daughter that it wasn't her fault if the baby cried or caused a lot of additional work.

Spending time with her

With any luck, spending time with your toddler should be easiest just when she needs it most – in those first few days when the baby's still very sleepy. There's no need to shadow your child like a private detective, but a few extra hugs and little chats may well be appreciated. On the other hand, they may not!

Hilda's son Toby seemed to react with complete indifference to Ben once he was home. And, he seemed less interested in his mother than usual – noticeable because he was typically rather a demanding child who preferred his mother's company to anyone else's. However, Hilda felt that he liked her to be near him, and spent many hours quietly reading in his room while he pottered about with his toys and baby Ben slept in another room. 'I had

67

the impression that he just wanted me around while his little brain thought it all through,' says Hilda, 'and after a few days he was much his normal self again. There were ups and downs with the baby – but I just see that as normal toddler bolshiness!'

Hilda's point is one it can be easy to overlook. If you're expecting jealousy, or a negative reaction, you have only to wait until the next time your toddler's in a bad mood. Don't forget she's rotten to everyone at times!

Keeping up routines

Trying to stick to your toddler's usual routines can be part of what makes you recover more quickly after a second birth. If you have to produce spaghetti for a small person at 12 noon sharp, you simply can't indulge in the massive disorganization of the first time round. The days of not getting dressed until 5 pm are over!

It is nice if routines are maintained for your toddler's sake, so that the arrival of the baby doesn't throw her whole life out of kilter, although she may well enjoy a day or two of relaxed anarchy with you. Lolling about in nightclothes and having exciting impromptu meals of ham and crisp sandwiches are an acknowledgement that something extraordinary has taken place – as indeed it has.

After the first day or so, however, try and have meals and bed at the usual time, and avoid any big changes, such as trying to make your toddler drop her daytime nap if she seems half-ready for it. This can be slightly more difficult if you have help around – Granny may believe in no nap and an earlier bedtime, for example – but on the other hand, it also means you will have more time to spend with your toddler. So, if you've always spent half an hour bathing her, reading to her and putting her to bed, do try and keep it up, and let someone else take care of the baby.

Outings can be more difficult in these early days, but perhaps it is possible to adjust them, rather than give them up altogether. For example, if you habitually take a half-hour walk, it can be trimmed to 15 minutes; a trip to the 'big shops' a mile away can be replaced by one to the small local shops at the end of the road. Some gentle exercise is good for you as well as for your toddler and of course the new baby will enjoy the fresh air, too.

Breastfeeding

Breastfeeding usually causes a toddler's eyes to pop out of her head as she tries to make out exactly what you are doing! Having that stare fixed on you can make you feel quite self-conscious as you try and position the baby correctly. Breastfeeding, more than anything else will make your toddler realize she has to share the attention on a very intimate level, so until she is more used to having the new baby around, try and give the first few feeds when she's not looking. More often the toddler wants to get in on the action, demanding a taste or at least a cuddle on your lap. If you want to give her a drop of milk on a teaspoon or finger to try, fine. Otherwise, you could distract her with her own drink, some special juice, for example, or chocolate milk in her beaker. Keep a few other items at your side, too – a little chair for her, books or other toys, felt-pens and paper, a biscuit, a potty and toilet paper. Tell her that once the baby's gone to sleep again, you'll have time to give her a cuddle – and do make good your offer even if by then she doesn't appear interested any more. Adult promises are remembered to the letter!

One ploy which often works, especially with little girls, is a suggestion that they feed their own 'baby'. In fact, many toddlers spontaneously copy their mothers, hitching up their vests and pressing a doll to their chests with what they consider to be the appropriate expression of intense concentration on their faces.

Your toddler's response

If you've been averagely organized about the first few days, your toddler's response may be surprisingly good. Laura reports:

> We were actually rather touched at the way Henry responded to Alicia. He did go a bit quiet for the first couple of days, but then he just seemed to love her. Of course, things might have been different if we hadn't had my mother-in-law around to help. I was able to spend quite a lot of time alone with Henry when I came home.

Most small children have a spontaneous delight in these beings smaller than themselves; even a child as young as 16 months may show an interest in babies, cuddling dolls and pointing to babies in the street, in picture books and even on nappy packs. Age can play a part in response. Henry for example was two, and continued to accept his sister without any real problems. An older child might not be as accommodating.

Elizabeth was four when baby Anthony arrived and, frankly, used to ruling the roost. Her mother Samantha had prepared her thoroughly for the event, but Elizabeth's first reaction on seeing Anthony was 'That baby's got horrible ears'. True, he wasn't the prettiest baby ever seen, but it often takes a few weeks to improve the looks of the average newborn and Samantha couldn't help being rather upset! Elizabeth, possibly sensing this, continued to make rude personal remarks about Anthony. Samantha ignored these for a while but finally lost her temper with her daughter. This was followed by tears, tantrums and finally a chat about Elizabeth's feelings.

It transpired that Elizabeth felt excluded, and felt she should be helping more with Anthony. Samantha did try and include Elizabeth more and now has some interesting photos which show Elizabeth completely dressing the bewildered but placid Anthony when he was one year old! The rude comments continued, but as she became more used to Anthony, these became teasing and finally affectionate.

In the last issue, however, reactions do depend on many factors: your toddler's personality, whether she's normally difficult or serene, antisocial or gregarious; how secure she feels in her relationship with you; whether there have been any other major life events, like moving, and so on. Even if your toddler doesn't appear to react very much to the baby, her general behaviour may still show some changes. She may be more fragile, crying and whining more easily than usual – hard to deal with when you're feeling a bit fragile yourself after a birth. However, do try and bite your tongue when this happens rather than give her a good scolding. Instead, do your best to praise anything you can, even if it's only what some psychologists call 'nearly-good' behaviour!

Mary's son Johnnie was what can only be called a real pain for about six weeks after the birth of baby Rose. Mary would try telling him off but was quickly stopped in her tracks by his pathetic cry of 'I want Mummy to be *pleased*!' It wasn't easy, but

Mary did her best to focus on all Johnnie's good points, even though her own mother said she was being too soft with him and giving in too easily. However, Mary's partner Bill supported her, feeling that gentleness would build up Johnnie's self-confidence in the long run. 'Don't get into battles with him,' was Bill's advice. 'Let him go as much as you can.' This seemed to be successful in that Johnnie did eventually settle down again, becoming his normal happy self, and appearing increasingly pleased with his baby sister.

Problems are dealt with more thoroughly in Chapter 9, but even in the short-term, be prepared for your toddler to regress, wanting to wear a nappy or drink from a bottle again. To help counteract this for now, try letting the toddler help with baby care, as Samantha did with Elizabeth. Even a two-year-old can easily help put cream on a bottom, fetch a clean nappy from a pack, and do up the tapes with a little discreet help from you. However, don't expect her always to be obliging when asked for help of this kind!

Finally, don't take your toddler's immediate reactions too much to heart if they're not all you'd hoped for. A few weeks may bring a very different story.

And the baby!

If you've read so far, you might be forgiven for thinking that having a second baby is no more than making sure your toddler is adequately managed! But, while your first child is angling for all the attention and reassurance she needs, of course you are quietly forming a fascinating new relationship with your second baby.

From the moment this new miracle is delivered into your arms, there is another person in your life – not just anyone, but someone whom you are going to know intimately. At this point, most of the worries about whether you'll be able to love a second child vanish!

There is something deeply satisfying in caring for a second baby because, so often, you don't have the itch of anxiety that went with the first. The desperate, heart-rending wail of a newborn no longer ties your stomach into knots; the whole relationship can have a special, peaceful quality to it (though some mothers with noisy second children might well disagree!)

It does have to be said though that some parents experience

flickers of disappointment about the sex of their second baby if they were hoping for something different this time round, especially if they plan for it to be their last child.

Rick knew he was being macho but couldn't rid himself of his desire for a son to follow Tina. Because of this, it took him a few days to adapt to the reality of baby Angela. Likewise, Hilda secretly longed for a dainty little daughter to follow Toby, but was landed instead with another enormous boy, Ben!

Needless to say, the parents adapted quickly enough to their new babies but it is worth acknowledging that such feelings, even if transient, do exist.

8
Everyday Life

The private life of a mother has a kind of illicit fascination when you're one of the species, even if there is nothing so tedious to the outside world. Every day you can see tea parties breaking up to the guilty accompaniment of, 'Oh dear, we've ended up talking about nappies again!' Or, washing, or feeding, or keeping tidy.

However, daily life with children *is* made up of these details, and a second baby does throw into chaos the routine that was so painstakingly established with your first child. Obviously, you don't want to invest too much energy in these details, but you do want to establish a new routine that will enable you to get on with life smoothly again. You need to find the best way of organizing yourself – not the way your friend over the road does it, but the way that suits *you*.

For the first few weeks – sometimes longer – a second baby does mean accepting a more restricted routine while you recover from the birth. You probably won't want to take your tiny baby out too much anyway; crowds generally lose their appeal at this time, especially if your toddler has a tendency to disappear into them at top speed! You may well be content to remain at home until everyone is more settled.

Even later on, however, it's true that everything is harder to accomplish with two children, and some of your activities may suffer. For example, if you used to take your toddler swimming, you may be upset to realize this will have to end because there's no crèche in which to leave the baby, or because she's still too small and unpredictable – never mind the added practical difficulties of getting two children ready! But this does change. In a few months' time, when the baby has settled into more of a routine, joint activities will be much easier. Meanwhile, look round for classes for yourself which do have a crèche, and start booking!

Breastfeeding too can seem to take up inordinate amounts of time, especially in the first weeks when many babies like to suckle on-and-off for most of the day. This is another reason why some second-time mothers like to give a bottle-feed or two a day – it's quicker. Constant breastfeeding can also leave you depleted and so you need to eat and drink well – and often. You may also feel less inclined to resume your normal activities again though breastfeeding mums are more mobile and travel light! (If you are having any problems, contact La Lèche League or the NCT – addresses at the back.)

On the other hand, if going out is that much harder, you may establish a home routine with two children sooner than you expect. Even if you happen to have a difficult baby, babycare itself is easier. You won't for example be breaking out into a sweat as you try and work out exactly how the baby fits into the sling. Wriggling a jumper sleeve over a tiny arm, with infinite care and frustration, will no longer take five long minutes. Because of your hard-won expertise from the first time round, handling another baby, with the gangling head and limbs, won't be so scary, even if you did experience a bit of stage fright when you picked your newborn up the first couple of times!

Many women also find day to day life easier because there is already an existing routine centring round the toddler, and the baby just has to fit in with this (as far as possible.) For example, if the toddler goes to nursery in the morning, the baby has to get dressed and have breakfast before you go; if the baby also sleeps in the pushchair or car on the way, you have a predictable time for her morning nap, too. Likewise, in the early days of looking after a baby, when random feeds endlessly merge into each other, the concept of the toddler's three meals a day can seem inspiredly simple.

Because this routine does already exist, some women find that their second baby grows up faster than the first – or seems to. With the example of the toddler ahead, the baby will certainly want to imitate the more advanced behaviour she sees, from eating cocktail sausages to sitting in vain on the pot, a wisp of toilet paper in each hand!

Getting out

As you quickly discover, there is an art to leaving the house with two children. Just as you're locking the front door, the toddler discloses an urgent need to go to the toilet, and by the time that's over the baby has filled her nappy or wants feeding. Most second-time mothers have their own private nightmare memories of outings that went wrong – a tantrum from the toddler in the doctor's to accompanying screams from the baby; joint, increasingly desperate grizzling while stuck in a traffic jam. Such occasions can damage the confidence of the most stalwart of mothers!

It is boring but ultimately more restful to remember the golden rule: don't attempt too much too soon. Start small and build up slowly – a cup of tea at a neighbour's, or a successful trip to the chemist's for nappies, are achievements enough in the early days. Aim for no more than one outing a day to begin with, and try and make it somewhere you can go on foot. If you haven't done so before, now could be a good time to research local resources – there may be some activity you've missed, or that you always meant to try but never did. Allow plenty of time to get ready at first – at least 20 minutes – and don't forget *you* have to assemble *your* belongings too. It sounds obvious, but it's all too easy, when you have at last got a recalcitrant toddler and fussy baby together, to forget and lock yourself out!

New mothers are traditionally not recommended to drive until four to six weeks after the birth, though of course it depends on you. Unless you feel very sure of yourself, however, do cut out the 30-mile drives to friends until you feel your new baby is more settled – that is, unlikely to demand an emergency feed on the hard shoulder. Be very sure you can cope with a new baby *and* a toddler who won't keep quiet for a moment. Constant prattling from the back can be very distracting, and it's a fact that screaming children in cars are responsible for some accidents. However, don't let this put you off – you do need to get out! If you never leave the house, your imagination may start to take increasingly desperate turns – that you've missed your vocation as an open-heart surgeon, for example, or that life would be better on a guava plantation in South America.

However, you may find that even after a few weeks you do need to be more structured about going out than before. To save yourself stress, one idea could be to allot a certain number of days per week to outings while you spend the other afternoons at home. Don't feel pressurized, and don't compare yourself with other people – go for whatever you feel you can comfortably manage. You can also help yourself by accepting the inevitable for a while and having plenty of activities to hand with which to keep your toddler content at home. Stock up with books or sewing or rugging for yourself, too –

anything that's easy to manage and can be put down and picked up again any number of times.

Ideas to try on a temporarily housebound toddler are:

- Get your toddler to act out nursery rhymes – provide props and costumes if need be.
- Plenty of extra books.
- A bag of special toys, kept on top of a cupboard, to be taken down one at a time.
- New clothes for the toddler's 'baby'. They don't have to be 'designer', squares of material with a slit for the head will do.
- Dressing up clothes for toddler – hats, gloves and bags, too.
- Natural treasure hunt in garden for leaves, grasses, flowers, snail shells etc – stick the results on a piece of paper.
- Impromptu doll's house made from cardboard boxes, furniture from matchboxes and empty packets, and tiny rag or pipe-cleaner dolls as inhabitants.
- Old photos of family – a constant source of fascination!
- The eternal cardboard box, big enough for toddler to sit in. You can even make a Wendy house out of a really huge box.
- Always have in the house: child glue and scissors, sellotape, paper, and non-toxic washable felt pens.

Shopping

Shopping, easy enough with one baby, is far more difficult with two. Oddly enough, this may not be so true in the very early days when the baby can go in a sling and the toddler sit in the trolley. Later though, when both toddler and baby have grown, load up the trolley with them both and you have a substantial weight to push even before you add the shopping! Some mothers actually heave-ho *two* trolleys round the aisles, one for children, one for shopping – a sight surely to bring a blush to the cheeks of the most anticrèche of managers.

It is irksome to spend your valuable free time on shopping, but if your elder child goes to playgroup or nursery, this may be the best time to do it. Look on it as an opportunity to relax and wander around with the baby without pressure. Or, ask your partner to do the shopping, or to mind the children while you go to the shops for a blissful child-free hour.

Keeping meals simple

Before you know it both children will be nibbling away at fish fingers and you'll have forgotten those early months when you tried to mash potatoes with a baby welded to the breast and an impatient toddler tugging at your skirt.

In the beginning, however, aim for meals which are nourishing but easy to serve for yourself, your toddler and your partner. Soon, the baby will be able to have some of them as finger foods, or puréed to make a first meal.

For example:

Raw foods: are often healthier and of course need no cooking. Salad possibilities are endless: cauliflower, pimentoes, chopped apple, sliced turnip, grated carrot, mushroom, beansprout, peas, beans, courgette etc, and serve with wholemeal rice or pasta, beans or new potatoes.

Frozen, packaged fish: the type that comes in compressed oblongs is easier to prepare than the real thing complete with guts and head. Just add lemon juice. Tinned fish is good, too.

Frozen turkey mince: is a useful standby, as are frozen turkey and rabbit chunks, frozen chicken pieces, and frozen liver.

Canned beans: there are many varieties (cannelloni, chickpeas, and haricot to name but a few) which can be served with anything from herbs or eggs to a saddle of mutton. Mash or purée them if they're not that popular and serve with tomato sauce.

Tomato sauce: to prepare to go with beans, pasta, and potato omelette, heat a tablespoon of olive oil, add a sprinkling of herbs and pepper then simmer a tin of tomatoes stirring occasionally.

Sandwiches: experiment using ordinary wholemeal bread or rolls, or wholemeal pitta bread. Nourishing fillings are: peanut butter, tuna fish, sardines, cottage cheese, prawns, lean beef, to combine with watercress, cucumber, tomato, celery.

Easy-to-prepare comfort bits: keep some for occasional days when you're all harried and miserable: cocktail sausages, oven-ready chips, jelly and icecream.

Chicken: very easy if you simply put it in the oven with butter, thyme and garlic, and can serve as one main meal with meat left over for salad and/or sandwiches.

Exercise

Although many mothers of small children like them to have at least one spot of exercise a day, it can sometimes be difficult to accomplish. Perhaps you still find it hard to organize an outing; perhaps you live further away than is convenient from the local park. Some toddlers, who are at nursery in the mornings, are past their best by lunchtime and quite honestly prefer to retire to their rooms for a rest or quiet play.

Exercise for them doesn't have to mean a plunge into the unlimited space of a park. If park expeditions are problematic, salve your conscience by setting aside a definite day or two a week for the struggle – or wait until weekends when your partner will be around. Or, go with a friend, or try and find someone who is willing to take your first child to the park for you. Otherwise, explore different kinds of exercise.

For example:

- Your toddler can walk with you to the shops, or to see a friend, or whatever other errands you go on.
- If you have a garden, turn your toddler out into it (childproof it first, of course) whenever you can.
- You could do bending, stretching and dancing exercises together to a tape of music.
- Yoga is another possibility; the flexibility of most small children makes them perfect candidates, and they also enjoy imitating the various animals which give their names to the poses (the Camel, the Cat, etc).
- On days when it's rainy or you just can't get out, try and set up one room as a playroom – invest in a smooth, wide plank of wood to set up against a bed as a slide, and perhaps you'd consider letting your toddler bounce on a bed that doesn't matter (surely most don't that much!)
- Family swimming sessions on Saturday mornings are hard work to organize but rewarding when you get there. You and your partner grab a quick swim each, let the children splash about, and then turn into the café for hot chocolate all round!

Bath time without panic

The easiest way to bath two children is together, right from the start, with the baby dipped briefly into the shallow end while the toddler plays in the deep end. It's a good way of forging the sibling relationship as well as saving trouble and water! Another way is to put the toddler in the big bath and bathe the baby in the baby bath on the floor – it depends on how closely you have to supervise your toddler in the bath, and on the size of your bathroom! Joint bathing doesn't suit everyone, though – the baby still so tiny and fragile needs all your attention, and you may feel you just can't manage the two of them at once, especially if your toddler is in a particularly venturesome mood that night. Some mothers prefer to stagger baths, the toddler one night, the baby the next. Children certainly don't need to have a bath every day, as a wash would do – for many it's an enjoyable way of winding down at the end of the day.

Standard advice at bath times is to have everything ready before you begin, but that can be easier said than done with a toddler who insists on removing the nightclothes from the bathroom, or dipping the towels in the bath, or floating his potty on the water. The answer is more shelves and/or more hooks! Now that you can't always be watching your elder child, you may need to make one or two alterations in your bathroom before you really feel organized.

Balancing everyone's needs

This sounds wonderful in theory. In practice, however, it probably means balancing the needs of baby and toddler in a wild kind of see-saw, while you and your partner struggle on as best you can! Don't worry, there will come a time when you find the four of you have settled down as a family, with a more manageable rhythm than in the early days.

There will be times when the routines of both children clash: when the toddler is demanding lunch, or help on the toilet, while the baby is screaming for a feed. Try not to let panic stampede you on such occasions, even though the joint noise can be quite appalling. Look on it as a case of all needs being equal, but some needs being more equal than others! You cannot give each child the same amount of attention at these times. Real life with two children is quickly placating one, whisking round to deal with the other, and turning back to the first. Not everyone will be happy with this kind of treatment. It shouldn't happen too often, though if it does, is there any way you could change your management of both children to make life easier? Is there an unresolved jealousy problem with the toddler? Has toilet training become too much of an issue between you and the toddler? Try and isolate specific problem areas so you can make any changes that may be necessary.

Perhaps one of the most difficult aspects of this time is not to become totally child-orientated. Try and make some time in which you and your partner can recover your positions as independent adults. It doesn't have to be an evening out at the opera each week – a child-free chat in the evenings can be a great sanity restorer. And, the occasional simple acknowledgement that this is a hard period of your lives does no harm. Hang on to the fact that the children will never be so small and demanding again: it does get easier!

It has been said that the main difference between one and two children is that with two you simply don't have a moment! But you do need time to yourself right from the beginning. It can be draining to turn round from finally putting baby and toddler to bed only to find your partner waiting to have a good old chew over his promotion prospects or the unspeakable insults offered him by a colleague at work.

However, part of not having time alone is how available you choose to make yourself. When you have finished putting the children to bed, you do actually have the choice between trundling downstairs to shake himself out of his television-induced trance, or sneaking into your bedroom for ten minutes relaxation. You don't have to rush from one situation to the next and, while you don't want to deny your partner's needs, yours need attention, too.

However busy you feel, there are usually some spots in the day which can be just for you, so long as you have the self-discipline to seize them. A few minutes for a solitary coffee, a prowl round the garden, or a bath, can be all that's needed to recharge your batteries. And, as both children grow older and more independent, you will be able to look beyond these modest ambitions, too!

Health

Perhaps you remember a time with your first child when you seemed to catch every germ he cared to bring home – with devastating results. This often happens when the child starts going to mother-and-toddler mornings or playgroups. As one doctor put it: 'The children pass on these bugs and because they're foreign to the household, the parents go down like ninepins!' This phenomenon does tend to repeat itself when the second baby starts getting out and about, and of course your toddler may be starting nursery school now, too, so be prepared – the 'out-of-house' bugs remain as potent as before!

It's also true that, as a second-time mother, you are likely to have less resistance than before, especially during the first year when both baby and toddler are still so demanding. This is why it is important to take your rest as and when you can, just as you did during pregnancy; to eat well, and exercise too, but not to overdo it. You need to be sensibly selfish about your health. Don't ignore warning signs, take them as messages from your body to slow down. This can sometimes be hard to do because you are so much in the habit of caring for your two children and your partner.

Laura, who had suffered an attack of gastroenteritis three weeks previously, had spent the day feeling rather sick but, with nothing worse to show than a bit of diahorrhea, she went ahead with a proposed visit to her grandmother 40 miles away, taking both children. She returned exhausted, and when she tried to get up early the next morning, she promptly fainted! The doctor diagnosed gastroenteritis again and dehydration – Laura hadn't wanted to eat the previous day and had forgotten to drink, too. The doctor advocated plenty of fluid, with glucose and salt solution. But the doctor's real prescription was advice to take it easy – advice more easily given than taken, perhaps, but none the less valid for that.

If the worst comes to the worst and the whole family is ill at once, you can at least all retire to bed and complain in company. It is unpleasant and lonely having to look after sick children while you yourself are ill, so make it as easy as you can:

- Take it very easy, entertain from your bed, like a grande dame of the eighteenth century.
- Get your partner to stock up on simple, comforting foods such as soup and chicken; better still, get him to take a day off work and help (so long as he isn't ill, too!).
- Make sure everyone drinks plenty of fluids.
- Accept any help that's offered from friends and neighbours.

81

- Let your children do all the things they're normally forbidden: children's television, constant snacking, etc.
- Be stupid – forget your responsibilities. Read a historical romance, cuddle up with your toddler for a junior video.
- When you're all better, consider going away together for a weekend so you recuperate faster – sea air is always sea air!
- Ask around for a couple of emergency childminders, women who don't mind caring for a child for a few hours without warning.
- If you are getting ill frequently, ask your doctor for help; or consider alternative medicine, such as homeopathic, where you may find advice about diet and general lifestyle helpful.

Holidays

No one would suppose, after going away with two children, that holidays are supposed to be for leisure, relaxation, and fun. You may retain a happy mental snapshot or two after the event. Maybe you remember the two of them scampering along the sands, faces aglow with the sea air, memory censoring the fact that it was a 7 am scamper; or the toddler singing to the baby on the motorway, memory censoring also the final, predictable fate of the cheap and cranky car on the long drive back.

In general it's true to say that holidays with two very small children are hard work. Those who are over-ambitious deserve everything they get, so think carefully before you embark. Your best friends may have found themselves in their converted barn in the Massif Central, but are you sure you want to spend two days listening to all those peculiar engine noises *en route*, and two weeks with bored, shivering children beneath a 15 foot roof that no central heating with reach?

It doesn't matter how organized you are, or how many sound books you read about travel with children. Stock up with books, apples, and cassettes all you like for that drive to France, and strap your children into their seats. By the time you reach Dover the pages will be gummed together with half-eaten fruit, the baby will have pulled out all the tapes, and the car seats, far from constraining them, will serve only as a kind of makeshift gymnasium for both. You, perched uncomfortably on the packed lunches in the back, will be feeling decidedly jaded from the combined impact of your partner's snarls about obstructed vision, and the effort of trying to stop both children at least from going through the car windows. In addition, in the flurry of getting off at 4.30 am to catch the first, cheapest boat, you are bound to forget something – one mother had to have her first child's comforter, a rug, sent to Grenoble from Surbiton by Red Star! One child may be manageable (more or less) on a long journey: two are not. Ambitious holidays with two bring out the beast in us all.

So, stay at Dover, or near it: go and find an oast house to rent, or a farm or bed-and-breakfast with babysitting services. Go no further than Normandy at most, and take another two-child couple with you so you can babysit for each other. Make the most of your hospitable mother-in-law. When your children are only a very little older, you'll be able to take advantage of all those holiday camps abroad which offer to take the children off your hands. But, with the best will in the world, a six-month-old baby and a two-year-old toddler just won't enter into the spirit of things with the club leader who would have them both be Junior Tigers.

It is possible to have peaceful times in places you would never have thought to search for peace: a holiday centre full of unremarkable chalets achieves new lustre because no cars or dogs are allowed, and there's a swing. If this sounds like arranging your holiday totally round the needs of the children, well, there are worse survival mechanisms. Part of life with two is managing the transition from taking a baby with you on *your* holidays, to finding holiday situations that two small children will enjoy.

9

Changes and Problems

It would be a mistake to attribute all of life's hiccups to the fact that you have had a second baby! Tantrums, overdrafts, and work disappointments will happen regardless of how many children you have. Nevertheless, your rhythm does change after a second birth; it's a time of transition, and can be unsettling for the whole family.

Your toddler is the one who will be affected most obviously. Her small world has been turned upside down by the arrival of a baby, and, once you've all settled down together at home, the reality of this may hit her. Even if she sailed through the first few meetings with the baby, it can take a few days for her true feelings to surface. Her reaction may be shown in a variety of antisocial ways, from a sneaky bite to a blatant forgetting of toilet training.

Before you blame every incident on the baby, however, do check to see if there is anything else going on in your toddler's life – she might be misbehaving because she's going through an unsettled phase at nursery, for example. (Of course, none of this may happen –your toddler may behave like a dream!) Her relationship with you is also likely to go through some changes; you both have to adjust to the fact that she isn't the baby any longer. You may be prey to guilt and worry about this, fearing that the toddler will be damaged by having to put up with second best. However, in the long run, it is healthier for the toddler not to monopolize you, and it won't be long before the baby starts to become another very real person in her life.

The problems caused by a second birth are not usually permanent, however infuriating they may be while you're going through them. By the time the baby is four to six months old, your toddler's initial reaction should be well over – even if another undesirable attitude has taken its place! Sometimes, a toddler's relationship with her sibling and/or family can go through an upheaval later on, when the baby is older – but at least then you're working within an established framework. There's more on this possibility in Chapter 10; this chapter concentrates on problems which are more likely to occur the first few weeks after the birth.

Your changing relationship with your toddler

When you come home with a second baby, one of the most poignant adjustments you have to make is in the relationship with your first child. You probably went through something like it after your first birth, when your relationship with your partner, and with yourself, underwent a deep transition. Having a baby alters your priorities like nothing else. Once you cross the great divide from childlessness to parenthood, everything is seen differently. With the new tenderness created by a baby, many parents find themselves for example unable to watch the news with the same detachment as before, especially if there is anything relating to children.

Letting go of someone who made such a terrific difference to your life can be difficult at times. You're used to worrying only about her – suddenly it's all much more rough and tumble. Your control has been eroded, and this can be deeply disconcerting for you and for her.

However, although you may feel you have obligations towards your first child, she isn't a duty. This kind of thinking can creep up on you unawares as you scurry from nursery to dance class to children's party. Will she be deprived if she doesn't socialize every day? Have I given her enough quality time today? Should she have a more advanced jigsaw or will I spoil her if I buy it? Guilt and worry about whether the toddler is getting your best are a natural part of parenting but shouldn't be allowed to shadow your pleasure in your child – in both children.

It may be helpful to bear in mind that letting go of your first baby is a process that happens anyway, whether you have a second child or not. That's the way nature designed it. The infant who was so totally dependent on you for food and warmth is very soon off on her own to a tea party with friends and, just a few years later, a week's camping with her school. This new independence starts to become noticeable around the three-and-a-half-years mark, when you may suddenly realize you haven't seen your child for half an hour or more because she's totally absorbed in an elaborate game about trains. Before this happy point is reached, you may unfortunately find yourself more irritable than before with your toddler, and this can be deeply upsetting for you both. It could partly be because you're still tired from the birth, or not quite well; and of course you have a new baby to look after, someone whom you don't yet know very well. Do consider asking your doctor for help – some extra vitamin and iron pills may be enough to make the required difference.

Bear in mind too that, because you've been accustomed to having just one child to worry about, her behaviour can seem more important than it really is. It's all too easy to become genuinely angry with your child over quite trivial pieces of behaviour – throwing toys or food, for example, or refusing to sit on a chair.

With a second child around, there is no longer the time or energy to focus on details, and it is the sense of strain created by this which can be so devastating, quite as much as the bad behaviour itself. With one child, you develop a habit of concern which can't really be carried over to second-time parenthood. Because you can't attend to your first child exactly the way you did before, you're likely to feel an increased sense of powerlessness which adds to the distress when your child doesn't behave properly.

Try not to expect too much of yourself as well as of your toddler. It is upsetting to realize that your beloved first child is arousing pure rage in you instead of pure tenderness, but didn't this happen before the second birth anyway? Try to accept that you won't be feeling loving towards her every day; young children still love and accept less-than-perfect parents, and of course you still love her, even if your feelings sometimes tell you different! Don't take total responsibility, or allow anyone else to foist responsibility on you, for her behaviour. Just do what you can.

It may also help if you can be a bit more detached. Don't forget that as your toddler grows older, some unruliness and disobedience can be quite healthy – she's asserting her growing independence, even if she sometimes seems to be getting to maturity via an unnecessarily tortuous route! Viewed positively, it may be good for her in the long run if the kid gloves come off a little more. As Laura's brother rather scornfully remarked when he saw her lose her temper with Henry: 'Oh, you're much better with him now. You used to let him get away with far too much!' The day may even come when a mother-of-one has the power to amaze you, with long drawn-out exchanges of the kind you now deal with far more briskly: a feeble reprimand as her child climbs over your tv, followed by a long, fruitless argument as to exactly why not, with the complete sabotage of all adult conversation and resulting exhaustion all round!

Supporting your child

Your response to your child's behaviour is important. Tolerance and understanding help: or, if you can't manage that, the ability to turn a blind eye is as good as anything! Make a resolution not to scold your child over the little things, and try not to punish her too much even if she seems to be asking for it; instead, praise what you can. This doesn't mean giving your toddler permission to get away with rampant bad behaviour; she does need limits. Just try not to become involved in fruitless emotional tussles.

Don't expect too much of a two-to-three-year-old. A child this age still needs your guidance. She needs the limitations which you alone can set down, whether that's bedtime at a reasonable hour or a ban on spitting in the house. Think of your child as needing your support during a difficult phase of her life, even if she seems to reject that support.

Regression

There is something peculiarly irritating and pathetic about the toddler who tries to imitate a baby, lying on her back, kicking her legs in the air and wailing. The crying is so patently false – one eye at least kept on you all the time – and the baby behaviour so blatantly put on, that your best aid is probably a sense of humour. Of course, some children are exceedingly sensitive about being laughed at, but do try your best to see the funny side. And, put yourself in her place. Don't we all like to regress at times?

It can also help to play along a little with her – after all, your toddler plays at being many other things besides a baby, and with a real baby around all the time, it would be surprising if she didn't make the most of the material to hand. So, let it be just one more game. Have a little basket with her own baby things in – an old herb container with talc, a nappy or two, a small bottle of baby lotion. Have some props for other games around, too, like cooking.

If this type of behaviour goes on and on, and looks like becoming an established part of your toddler's life, you can try and chivvy her gently out of it. Point out that babies are in fact rather boring – or at least lead a relatively boring life! They can't enjoy many of the privileges of an older child, like running round the park or eating a bun. Perhaps you could reinforce this point by letting your toddler have some novel treats, like a later bedtime or permission to watch a special television programme.

Continued regression may also be a sign that your toddler is underchallenged. Is there another activity she could take on? Could she start nursery school a bit earlier? Look round for something that will boost her status as 'a big girl'. Specific signs of regression, like wanting a bottle or soiling, need casually tactful handling. For the first few weeks it might be an idea to buy the toddler a bottle for herself, but on your terms. Lay down a few ground rules from the start, to stop it attaining the status of a comforter: the bottle is not to be taken to bed, or on outings, and has to be put away with the rest of the toys before bedtime. The toddler can have milk in it once a day, water the rest of the time. Later, when the toddler's interest wanes, you can throw the bottle out – or suggest she uses it to feed her dolls with.

Wetting and soiling are more annoying to deal with especially if, like Mary's son Johnnie, your child always seems to perform while visiting other people.

Annoyed though she was, however, Mary did her best to bite her tongue and keep her reactions. 'I found that if I got angry, it honestly didn't help much. I would simply clean him up and remove him to another room while I disposed of the mess, so that at least he didn't have the satisfaction of witnessing all the activity he'd caused.' Mary also went back to some of her potty-training ploys – reminding Johnnie more often to go to the toilet, and praising or rewarding him when he did.

If your accident-prone child is very recently out of nappies, you could try putting her back in them, if only for outings. In a child this young, maturity comes and goes before becoming really established. Also, genuine accidents are a part of a toddler's life – she may simply forget to go because she's too absorbed in what she's doing.

Tantrums and bad temper

The creative toddler can demonstrate a truly impressive range of nasty behaviour. Sulks, bolshiness, and disobedience can all be part of a warm-up programme which explodes in the full-blown tantrum,

with screaming, hitting and destructive behaviour. Such demon-
strations are part of a toddler's life but can take on new significance
after the birth of a second baby.

Don't reward your toddler with too much attention; one ploy is to
put her into another room to cool off for five minutes, and then
administer comfort when the worst of the storm has blown over, like
Penny:

> I found that the problem was fuelled by the fact that I was no
> longer always immediately to hand to sort out problems before
> they became too frustrating. Sometimes, William needed me to
> defuse the behaviour which leads up to a tantrum, and, if I was
> busy with Davina, I wasn't always quick enough!

If your first child is exploding rather often, try giving her more of
your undivided attention – reading, cuddling, talking. Try not to
attend to the baby in one room, while the toddler's heating up next
door; bring the baby in and change him on the floor.

It's a fine balance. On the one hand, you don't want to increase
any feelings of insecurity related to the birth of the second baby; on
the other hand, your child also has to learn that she sometimes has
to wait for your attention, and that you can't spend your life running
after her whenever she gets into trouble. Teach her that you will
come to her when you can, even if that isn't always when she
demands. Be specific about this: 'Wait until I've done up this
nappy', rather than: 'Hang on a minute!' Then go to your toddler at
once, so she learns you will help when you say you will.

If your child has developed the bad habit of yelling for you to
come from another room, you can also ask her to come to you
instead; if need be, enforce the request by ignoring those shouted
commands for your presence. With lesser bad temper – whining,
disobedience, and so on – it's probably best to ignore it as much as
possible. You can also try laughing your child out of it, or distracting
her with a new activity. Don't threaten a child with punishment, but
point out dispassionately what the results of her actions will be. For
example, if she won't put on her socks, then she won't be able to go
to the park.

Samantha coped with Elizabeth's whining by telling her that if
she went on, Samantha would get a headache and wouldn't be

able to read to her at bedtime. As Elizabeth loved her books, that was often enough to keep her quiet!

Assaulting the baby

Never ignore toddler attacks on the baby. Hitting, biting and any hurtful behaviour to the baby (including accidentally-on-purpose clumsiness) must be nipped in the bud. Apart from anything else, your toddler just won't feel happy with herself if you allow her to get away with it. This kind of behaviour is often experimental, so you must make it absolutely plain that, no, just as she suspected, it is not all right. Tell your child firmly and clearly that biting and hitting hurt, and are not allowed, but don't bite or hit her to prove your point – all you will do is hurt her. If she persists, put her in another room for a few minutes to reinforce the message, although your disapproval and the baby's crying will probably be enough to cut this type of behaviour short. In fact, the toddler is just as likely to frighten herself as the baby (especially if he lets out a piercing scream upon being bitten!) and may need comforting once the telling-off is over. This also applies of course if she has hurt the baby accidentally – make a distinction between deliberate spitefulness and the injury that might be caused by any boisterous toddler who enjoys throwing cushions about. And of course there are also those more questionable 'accidents', when the toddler just can't help bumping into the baby or pushing him over. Be sensible, don't leave baby and toddler alone together until the baby is big enough to sit up and repulse any unfriendly attempts, which won't be for at least six months. Even then, it probably isn't wise to leave the two alone for too long – guage the emotional temperature for yourself.

Jealousy

What do you do if your child does turn out to be jealous after all? If she whinges every time you go to the baby, or says she doesn't like the baby and wants to send him back? First, it helps to accept it as a natural reaction, and not to feel that it's a sign of failure on your or on her part. To put it in perspective, the baby may surprise you in a few months' time by showing signs of jealousy too! 'Angela at ten months would try and push Tina off my lap, and scream when she had to share cuddles!' says Susan.

Although jealousy is often obvious, it can be difficult to identify as such, or to isolate it from a whole range of difficult behaviour. Don't analyse your child's behaviour endlessly but, if you suspect she is jealous, aim at being generally supportive and gentle. Perhaps she could have a few extra little treats at this time – a phone call to Gran, a special outing with her father, a new book, an extra cuddle in your bed at night.

Because you're busier than you were before, it can be surprisingly hard to find an uninterrupted chunk of time to give your child, even if the baby is napping. It's hard to get into reading Postman Pat for the 49th time when a day's washing up is calling, but don't allow your time with your child always to be overshadowed by some impending task. The jobs will still be there when your child has gone to school.

Should you modify your behaviour towards the baby if the toddler is very jealous? It would be very hard if you had to restrain yourself from kissing the baby simply because your toddler was there. Perhaps the best option is just to give the toddler a kiss, too! It isn't really a question on cutting down on the attention you give the baby so much as making sure you can give your first child all the love and reassurance she's asking for.

Attention-seeking behaviour

It is amazing how often your toddler requires emergency attention during a nappy change or breastfeed. Suddenly, she's got to have a drink, or a trip to the toilet, or there's a toy that just has to be found if life is to continue.

Try asking your toddler if she wants anything before you turn your attention to the baby; then try and interest her in some activity. However, this won't always work neatly with some aspects of babycare and you may just have to play it by ear. Bathing a baby can take a good 20 minutes, for example, and in this case, your toddler will just have to wait, as you can't leave a baby in the bath. Again, many breastfeeds do last a long time and you can't really expect your young child to amuse herself quietly for the whole of this time. Just break off occasionally to deal with the most pressing of her needs; better still, make an effort to settle her beside you before you start to feed.

Toddlers do go through phases of asking you to 'come and see' ten times in a row when they're excited about some activity they're engaged on – making a doll's hat out of a sock, or a bird's nest out of odd twigs, for example. This gets rather wearing after about three times – try shouting out your admiration loud and clear instead, so long as it doesn't frighten the baby!

Of course, your child needs your admiration – who will come and see if you don't? However, you may have to introduce clearer limits if your child starts to display bad temper in an attempt to get your attention away from the baby. Your child's mood can provide a useful rule of thumb – so long as she's happy and obliging, there's no reason why you shouldn't give her all the attention she needs.

Mannerisms

The toddler may sometimes greet the baby's arrival with the introduction of the nervous sniff or cough. Face-pulling and nail-biting are other possibilities. There may just be some physical reason for these (e.g. her nose is blocked) otherwise, mannerisms are best left to melt away quietly on their own, with as little attention drawn to them as possible.

When one child is disabled

It is easy for the dynamic of a family to revolve around a disabled member. A disabled first child may be especially put out by the arrival of a sibling, and may need even more reassurance than usual. Likewise, an older child may find herself unexpectedly neglected if the baby turns out to be disabled; even a minor health problem in a new baby can be very worrying for parents, and easily drain all their attention.

It needs extra self-discipline to deal with a naughty toddler if she is disabled; but just like other children, she does need limitations in order to feel safe. If a disabled first child is allowed to get away with what you know to be bad behaviour, there may come a time later in life when she exerts a subtle form of bullying over her siblings in order to get her way: a situation can arise in which the whole family tends to give in because of her disability.

If the baby is disabled, it will take additional effort to make sure the toddler doesn't suffer unfairly as a result of all the anxiety and practical arrangements that ensue. Clear explanations of what has happened will help. Small children tend to think that the world revolves around them, and that they are responsible for anything out of the ordinary, so do give your first child all the reassurance you can. Your child will be more worried by your attitude than by the baby himself.

It is unfortunately beyond the scope of this book to explore disability in more detail, but do have a look at the Address section at the back for further help and advice and at another Sheldon title *A Special Child in the Family* by Diana Kimpton.

Neglecting the baby?

According to some, this is a real – if rare – possibility. In an anxiety to appease the toddler, parents can sometimes overlook just how much attention tiny babies need. However, it is misleading to think of neglect by itself. It's probably more true to say that with two children, your attention needs constant balancing, and, at times, one or the other will demand more than you can give. You may occasionally find that the baby has to wait for a feed because the toddler is sobbing desperately after a fall, or because you're in the last throes of putting her to bed. Or, the baby may not be getting enough milk because you are having feeding problems – perhaps the baby isn't positioned correctly on the nipple, for example, or you have worn down your supplies by too much running around.

All this is quite different from neglect. If you do feel the toddler – who is after all older, more powerful, more verbal and more manipulative – is taking more than her fair share, or that the baby is not receiving all he needs physically or emotionally, discuss it with your partner to see if you can establish a new balance. It's true that you can sometimes feel awkward or even guilty at paying the baby attention if a bolshy toddler is in the vicinity; on the other hand, there's certainly no need for a baby to be left crying in order to prove how much you love your first child!

10

Later On:
A Growing Relationship

As time goes on you discover to your joy that two children become far more of a unit. They have meals together, baths together and bedtimes together – or almost! With the second baby, the milestones that so delight parents first time round – sitting up, crawling, walking, independent feeding – take on extra meaning because they mark the way to the baby joining the family in earnest. After a few months, she is no longer an alien being, with incomprehensible routines, and different food, but a recognizable child fast catching up with her elder sibling. One year on, life will be very different from the chaos of the first few post-natal weeks.

Don't forget that the toddler as much as the baby will be growing up quickly in this first year, and will also become easier to look after. With any luck, the worst of the terrible twos will be over and he may have mastered valuable skills like retrieving his coat from the heap at the bottom of the stairs, or rendering you an accurate account of his nightmares. During this period, he may grow out of having a nap, removing one extra complication in your day; or perhaps he'll leave off night nappies. He may learn to dress himself, set the table, tidy his room, and even wash his hair – up to a point.

The stage where the new baby's routine clashes with the toddler's at every point seems to go on for ever at the time – and then suddenly it's over. After months of the baby falling asleep when you want to go out, or demanding lunch at your toddler's naptime, the baby catches up. The day she clambers on to the toddler's chair and starts poking about his plate signals the arrival of a whole new phase!

Now you start learning the qualifications of the old chestnut that life with two children is easier. Life with an older baby and an older first child *can* be easier *at times*. How much older? This does depend on individual circumstances, of course, but generally, once the baby is over six months old, it gets better, and after the baby hits her first birthday, better still! Of course, the difficulties of this period do also depend on the age of your toddler, and on the temperaments of both children. A calm older child approaching four is likely to be much less hard work than an excitable two-year old in the throes of daily tantrums.

Once the baby is big and strong enough to repulse any attempts at actual bodily harm by the toddler, you may find you can take a bath alone, without interruptions, for the first time in years, while they amuse themselves in another room. On the other hand, your idyll may be rudely broken in on by shrieks of distress as a life-or-death battle breaks out over a Lego brick. However, this is the beginning of a relationship. Just when you feel you can't take another minute of hit-and-run behaviour on both sides, you're swept into a new dimension by seeing two little forms bulging from behind the curtain and knowing that they have made a truce, however temporary; or by seeing the baby's face generously smudged with the toddler's ice cream; or by hearing the toddler offer violence to Aunt Nelly for accidentally bumping into the baby. Don't be surprised at the almost ferocious protectiveness of the toddler towards the baby – even if they don't seem to get on well, let he who dares approach that pushchair!

From the toddler's point of view, an older, more responsive baby is great fun: and, for you, a valuable means of absorbing attentions that might otherwise come your way for as much as 12 hours on the trot. The baby provides an uncritical listener to strings of songs and nursery rhymes; will willingly act as the spider should your toddler want to be Miss Muffet; and, soon, will take turns at doing belly flops onto the sofa. The toddler in his turn can provide you with valuable information on the baby's state of mind – running to tell you that she's woken from her nap as you're sunbathing in the garden, and giving matter-of-fact interpretations of her different cries: 'Wants some chocolate!'

More settled though their behaviour is, however, it still can't be relied upon. On some nights, a sleepy toddler will help the baby to settle quickly, or vice versa; on other nights, both will be wakeful and mischievous. A hungry toddler may encourage a fussy baby to try some new food; or he may copy the baby's demonstration of how to throw a Marmite sandwich. Around this point you realize that the initial problems may have gone, but that you are faced with a new one: the question of discipline, and no longer just for the toddler, either. You may need to tell the baby off for pulling the toddler's hair, or for screeching instead of sharing a toy, or for barging in on your toddler's bedtime read with her own book. While this may herald the opening of a welcome phase as far as the toddler is concerned, the last thing you want is to get your children into some kind of competition for your approval. You may feel this has happened if your elder child starts openly preening himself about how good and capable he is in comparison with his younger sibling. This can just be part of your child's developing awareness of the implications of his behaviour, but if you're not sure, try giving him an extra dose of love and reassurance. Sometimes, constant insistence on his own good qualities can indicate he feels unsure of his lovability, especially when there is another child around to share the attention.

Generally, though, the basics of discipline with two are the same as with one: consistency, not giving too many commands, and praising and rewarding good behaviour. Don't worry about being completely, scrupulously fair so long as you feel your general attitude is seen to be consistent as far as is practicable. Obviously, you still can't expect as much from the baby as from the older child, and even when they're older both children will have different needs at different times as far as direction of their behaviour is concerned. Both in the future and now, they need to be treated as individuals.

When the novelty wears off

'At first, we were all thrilled,' recalls Hilda. 'Toby accepted Ben with hardly any fuss and really seemed to love him – spent ages hanging over his cot making faces at him and kissing his toes. Then, when Ben was about four months old, Toby just did an about-turn. Every five minutes, it was "I don't like that baby. Throw him in the bin!" '

Hilda's experience is that of some families who find that, after an initial good start, problems between toddler and baby can crop up at a later stage – six months or even a year later. The excitement of the birth is over, and everyone has become used to having an extra member of the family. In addition, as the baby becomes bigger and more mobile, she may start pulling the toddler's hair or poking her fingers too near his eyes; or she may start to grab his toys. She's no longer a passive little bundle to be admired from a distance, but a living entity with whom your toddler has to share space!

Also, you may experience the sibling relationship as more

difficult because the novelty has worn off for you, too. At some point after a second birth you may begin to feel that it's all drudgery. More on your feelings in the next chapter!

Now could be a good time to re-assess your whole lifestyle since the birth of the second baby. Does your routine revolve round the baby a little too much? When you sit down to play with your first child and the baby blunders in, is she allowed to interrupt the game? Because you're so much busier with two, are you constantly asking your toddler to 'Just wait until I've done . . .' before you can attend to him? Are you too hemmed in to take him out as often as he'd like? Or, has the toddler been allowed to get away with too much? Write down areas of dissatisfaction, along with anything you could do to improve them.

Whatever rosy visions you may have about your two children sharing everything, it's a fact that small children are often highly possessive about their belongings. Your toddler may also be at a stage where imaginative games are deeply real and he finds it unbearably frustrating to be interrupted. Just when he's spent half an hour creating a special brick barn for his toy animals, along comes the baby and knocks it down in seconds. What self-respecting artist wouldn't raise a protest?

It is true that learning to get on with other people is an important part of your first child's life, and he can't be shielded from this all the time. However, a toddler who is suffering from this kind of delayed jealousy may well appreciate just a little re-arranging of affairs.

For example, you could try and make your toddler's 'own place' – somewhere he can go and play secure in the knowledge that the baby isn't allowed in. If he has his own bedrooms it could be out of bounds to the baby, perhaps just for certain times of the day. Otherwise, a hut at the bottom of the garden, a corner of the utility room, behind a sofa, or simply a blanket draped over a table, can all provide private space. If by now your older child is going to nursery every day, he will probably need some time on his own afterwards, just as you relish a quiet cup of tea after a hard day's work yourself!

The sibling relationship will not flourish very well if the baby is allowed to damage the toddler's toys and books. This may mean a tedious phase of physically removing the baby from the danger zone. Make the most of the fact that she is still easily distracted and will be just as happy with some old plastic cups of yours, as the set the toddler has painstakingly arranged for a doll's tea party.

It can be tempting to throw all the responsibility for this stage on to the toddler. 'Just give it to her for a moment! You must share!' are words that easily spring to the lips. Because the baby is smaller and more defenceless, your maternal impulse will be to shield and protect her from the more able older child – being a fair mother becomes much easier when the baby has lost some of that wide-eyed innocence and starts to pout angrily and smack back instead!

Meanwhile, remember, your first child isn't that old yet, and the baby shouldn't be allowed to dominate too much. Of course, the toddler does need to learn how to play with other children without tears; a willing sharer will find life that much easier. And, he must understand that the baby too has to have toys and attention. However, left to himself, he will probably be quite happy to let the baby have both – in his own time and in his own way!

Involving the toddler

Making sure the toddler isn't excluded from babycare can be quite easy the first few days when you're content to sit back and let your first child stroke the baby's face or fetch a clean nappy from the bathroom. It becomes harder when you want to speed up and get impatient with your toddler for smearing cream all over the nappy straps, making them impossible to do up. Your first child is so much slower and more easily distracted than you, that his 'help' is often more trouble than it's worth, though obviously it's important not to quash his little efforts. Involving the toddler goes beyond letting him make a mess of the occasional nappy, however. It's a question of a whole attitude on your part. How far do you want to – or can you – keep the baby separate from the family? First time round, there was a baby's room, with baby's clothes and cotton wool etc. This time, matters are more blurred; you may come up to put the baby to bed to find the toddler napping in the cot.

The second baby is a member of a ready-made family in a way that a first baby is not. So, make the most of this. Do let the toddler 'help' with as many aspects of babycare as possible (reminiscent of those Victorian elder sisters who brought up siblings ten years or so their junior!). A toddler can rock a baby in the pram; can help wash the baby; can make her laugh by playing pee-bo; may be able to quieten a crying baby by singing or by jiggling her bouncing cradle.

By letting your toddler take the initiative and discover, to his delight, his power to entertain the baby, you can start to pave the way to a close sibling relationship. The attitude of the elder child has a great deal of influence as to the future of this relationship, especially in the first two years of life, so give your first child some freedom in which to be creative around his younger sibling, even if you're watching to make sure that creativity doesn't get out of hand! Absence can be used to involve the toddler, too; for example, if the older child goes to nursery, you can tell him that the baby has been wondering where he was when you go to collect him. Very soon this will become true: not only will the baby be looking round for her absent sibling, you will probably find the older baby alone harder work than when the toddler is there to amuse her!

Fostering the sibling relationship

To some extent, ensuring that your children become friends is a matter of chance and temperament. However, perhaps one of the main ways in which you can help is by not trying too hard. Let them find their own path without being made to feel that they are acting some game of comradeship all the time before your approving eyes. Of course you must watch the toddler when the baby is still very small, but once the baby can walk and shove, it is an idea not to rush in and sort out every one of their squabbles. Evolving the right balance of power is something both children need to learn for themselves. Leaving the children alone can in fact be a way of promoting good relations – you may find that the quarrels break out only on your return! Your own judgement will direct you as to when you can safely do this. The best time to slip out is when the toddler is happily engaged in some make-believe game of his own, and the baby engrossed in her separate toys. The older child will probably chat away quite happily to the baby about his game, although children this young won't really play together. Under twos are much more interested in exploring the world around them than in actively playing with another child, and it may not be before your second child is three that you can expect them to sustain games together. The happy time will come when they're too busy being pirates upstairs to come down for lunch!

Enrolling the older child as teacher can also help; the toddler can show the baby how to do something, like building a tower of bricks, or wrapping up a doll in a blanket. Even if the baby can't copy the toddler yet, her attention will still be held for long enough to flatter the toddler into further instruction! And, if imitation is the sincerest form of flattery, the baby will be doling out plenty as soon as she becomes more mobile – dancing when the toddler dances, shouting when he does – a double act which represents the beginnings of playing together.

As the needs of your two children change, you can give them further opportunities to become closer. For example, if the toddler and baby haven't shared a room, you might consider letting them do so when the baby is older – six months old, a year, 18 months. It doesn't really matter when – when it feels right to you.

When three-year-old Tina went through a phase of having nightmares, Susan promised that baby Angela could come in to keep her company. Susan had hesitated to put them together because Tina's room was rather small, but found that both Tina and Angela, now nine months, enjoyed sharing. An unexpected bonus was that, whereas previously Angela's bedtime had been quite erratic, she now usually settled within minutes of her sister.

New privileges for the toddler

Between two and five years is a time when children grow up fast, both intellectually and physically. From one week to the next you may find that your child is speaking in clearer, more complex sentences, or that his legs look thinner because he's grown an inch or so.

At some point during this time you'll probably feel it's appropriate to start treating your elder child in a slightly more grown-up way. Of course, you want to treat both children equally when it comes to sharing out the chocolate drops, but both children do have different needs. For example, you might want to give your elder child a later bedtime story so you can read him the more complicated books the baby doesn't appreciate. Or he could start a mini-gym class which would be too advanced for his sister, or attend a party on his own, or stay overnight with a friend. It's no longer a matter of placating the elder child with treats because he's jealous of the new baby, but of recognizing that his needs are changing and growing all the time, and that the two children can't be treated entirely *en bloc*.

100

11
What About You?

As far as you yourself are concerned, some things are helpful after you have had a second baby: any remnants of the extended family; paid help; a lavish supply of local friends; a really effective washing machine; a steady flow of spare cash; a reliable car. These matters are not always under your control. But more fundamental than all these is the inner confidence that you have made a valuable and life-enhancing decision in going ahead with another baby.

This ingredient, while more malleable than others, can prove elusive at times, but is important in an era where it can be easy to lose sight of yourself and your personal aims. At base, of course, the fulfilment offered by a second baby is quite as generous as most of us hope. Nevertheless, the emotional aftermath of this second arrival is complex and longlasting. No one wants to be negative about the impact of a second baby, but for many women, the reality does involve some emotional adjustments. It can be a challenging time as you struggle to re-define your identity in a way which takes account of your growing family without leaving you swamped by it.

What strikes many second-time parents is the sheer overwhelming nature of life with two small children, especially in the early days. 'But – how are you supposed to manage? I just don't have a moment to myself', was the faint complaint of one bewildered father. Because of this lack of personal space, it's easy to start feeling worn down and resentful. However, it is important, as much as possible, not to let these feelings escalate into a habit – that way martyrdom lies! Discipline yourself to hang on to some selfishness.

You could learn here from assertiveness training, which typically postulates a clear, specific, but non-aggressive request for your rights to be met. This might involve making sure you or your partner leaves work on time, even if office mores tacitly demand you hang around afterwards. Or, you might want to ask your partner to do more: 'I feel I need Tuesdays to be my night off while you bathe the children and put them to bed, how do you feel about this?' Or it could be showing your first child more definitely that you too have needs: 'Mummy will read to you after she's had her cup of tea. Right now she's tired and needs to have a little rest'.

In the first few weeks, some women can feel overwhelmed by the reality of their task – having to wade through all the hard work of a young baby's life for the second time. Just when your first child is becoming reasonably human – toilet trained, more independent about dressing, eating and play – you've got it all to go through again, this time without the excitement of novelty, and with more knowledge of what lies ahead! All those unspeakable nappies, all the grinding anxiety of those colds, the whole rigmarole of teething – it was hard enough first time round when there was only one. How are you going to cope now that you have two?

Little by little, is probably the best answer. As noted before, second babies *are* often more placid than first ones, and the chances are that it will all flow more easily – it's just the prospect of it which seems so overwhelming. Break it down. Can you manage today? If not, can you manage for half of today, or for the next hour or even five minutes? Try not to look too far ahead, life never turns out the same as our imaginings. Give yourself time – once you have really come to love your second baby, it will all seem far less daunting.

Later, when those first chaotic weeks are over and you've all settled into a routine, you can feel oppressed by the limited nature of life as imposed by two small children. Because it's that much harder to arrange childcare and go out, you can feel that your world has shrunk, your interests dwindled. The details of mothering are no longer a problem, but what about your lifestyle? In this case, some changes might be called for, such as a return to work, or a conscious effort to improve your social life. Or the change could be in your own attitude – a recognition that the children won't be this small for ever, and that it's best simply to enjoy them while this phase lasts.

If you do have the inner confidence to abide by your decision in mind as well as in fact, you can develop the resources to obviate or sidestep some of the classic dissatisfactions of being a mother in our society. You may well feel that a second child brings into sharper focus issues like the limited recognition of motherhood, and the relative lack of acknowledgement, status, and pay, attached to what is most indisputably work.

However, according to recent research, many women increasingly feel that to be indignant about these archaic though slowly changing attitudes, is to be indignant on society's terms – even to risk being behind the times themselves. They feel that the certainties of feminism, effective though their foundation work has been, no longer offer totally satisfying answers in a world of increasingly complex economics as well as growing confusion about gender and roles.

Certainly, unless you are burning with some world-changing crusade, to evolve your own terms on which to face life involves less energy, and is more pragmatic as a mother of two. Many women seem to be experiencing a swingback from traditional feminist demands to an attitude which takes more account of women's rights to stay at home and supervise the bringing up of their children, often with the financial support of work they themselves have created, rather than the male-structured nine-to-five job. More on work in the next chapter!

All in all, a second birth isn't something you get over in order to return to normal as soon as possible. You are faced with the task of creating a new normality, which is the more unsettling because you have already re-created your life once before, around the needs of your first child. With a second baby, work, leisure, self-image – all need rethinking again.

Your identity – just a mum?

It is interesting how a busy second-time mother can feel politely ignored by life. Some women feel an unease at sinking into motherhood, a kind of guilt that they have only brought a second child into the world instead of running off to create management training programmes or to campaign for the suppression of Rottweillers. While presidents have been making decisions and the stock markets have been rolling, you have been hunting for the last clean nappy and trying to puzzle out exactly which nursery rhyme it is that your toddler is so desperate to recite to you. It certainly helps if you can reconcile ambivalent social expectations of motherhood with your own feelings. As Laura complains:

Two children seem to act as a label in the way one doesn't – a 'mother-of-two' is the stock norm which society expects to see, and all too often no further identification is presumed necessary! No one has ever asked me: 'And what do you do?' or 'What hobbies do you have?' when I've got them both tucked into the pushchair!

Women like Laura, who have always worked, may find some kind of private enterprise the most satisfactory way to face a society in which both men and women are increasingly uncertain about what they should be doing in terms of work and family. (In fact Laura, as we shall see in the next chapter, did start up her own business, though of course it doesn't have to be a matter of paid work.)

Like Laura, you may feel that the satisfactions of having two children are indubitable, but that they are private satisfactions; there are few pats on the head from the outside world. The knowledge that you are doing a worthwhile job is more dependent on your own inner strength, your intrinsic identity, than on feedback from external sources. This is why supportive friends and outside activities are so important – they provide a valuable reflection of yourself when society in general won't provide the mirrors!

But, other women find this one of the happiest times of their lives. They can see the fruits of all their hard work in their growing toddler, and they have another beautiful baby, whom they find much easier to handle second-time round. Penny, who followed up William with Davina, comments:

Because my second baby has been so perfect, it's really got me wondering about a third. She's growing up so fast – the second time around, it all seems to go much more quickly. I feel really reluctant to see this part of my life go.

Penny does add that her contentment has something to do with being able to afford a part-time mother's help to clean and babysit:

Also, I feel a lot of it is down to the temperament of your baby – I was lucky because mine is so placid.

Sexual relations are another aspect of life which for many women are not so much changed as suspended for some time after a second birth. This does happen after a first child, but seems to last longer after a second! 'You just don't get round to it!' was the blunt observation of one mother, echoed with varying shades of delicacy by other second-time parents who feel that fatigue and the ambience of two children just isn't conducive to feats of high passion. This can lead to anxieties about coldness and rejection

104

between partners, because sexual closeness is so easily equated with emotional closeness. You may feel that if lack of physical contact has been going on a long time, it becomes increasingly harder to break that barrier, but don't worry, you're not the only one! If you don't want to wait for things to right themselves, perhaps a talk between you and your partner would be enough to help. Otherwise, it's only pragmatic to take advantage of other people's help, so do consult your doctor or a marriage guidance counsellor.

Feelings of growing older may creep in for the first time around this point – the tummy that's been stretched twice now, the first grey hairs, the overall feeling that you are visibly becoming A Mother, with perhaps shades of maternal plumpness! While we all need to learn how to grow older gracefully, it is important not to fall in with your image of yourself if you don't like it. Your signals to the outside world – clothes, hairstyle, posture – are all up to you. If you feel you want to change but aren't sure how, why not rope in a friend? You can turn out cupboards and swap clothes together, go to the hairdressers' and attend yoga classes together!

It can help enormously if you have some source of identity which is independent of home. This can range from a friendly grand-mother you can visit in the evenings, to a full-blown executive post which doesn't leave you a thought for anything else while you're there. It could be involvement with a charity, or with a social or arts centre, or a political movement – any activity which offers a chance to develop a self-image outside of the family and avoid the 'mother-of-two' syndrome! In practice, this can be difficult to achieve because of the nature of life with two very small children, certainly at first. It becomes impossible not so much to start any activity, as to be sure of continuing with it, or finishing it. A second-time mother's life is littered with beginnings.

Not being able to rely on having the time or energy to finish anything can become demoralizing over a period of time even if you feel you can cope at first. It is tiring to live in a half-tidy, more or less clean state; to start art and singing classes and give up after three goes because you're just too tired. The best answer is probably to attempt less. This phase of skimping and untidiness will not last for ever.

At some point, some mothers have to question whether their feelings are sliding into post-natal depression. If you had it the first time round, you may be worried about whether it will recur. With normal post-natal depression, it isn't really known whether this possibility is more or less likely. There *is* a higher likelihood of developing post-natal psychosis – if you had it previously you have around a 30 per cent chance of getting it again – but it must be emphasized that true post-natal psychosis is extremely rare. If you do start to feel depressed, take action as soon as you can – don't let your feelings paralyze you. Consult your doctor and/or the Association for Post-Natal Illness (see Addresses.)

Another reason that you may be feeling swamped by motherhood is because your toddler is now becoming a big child, and your thoughts may even be turning to school. You may be in the process of realizing new responsibilities as a parent, concerns that didn't occur when that toddler was a baby. You realize that there is more to it than picking out a babygro for the day and wondering when to start him on solids. Emotionally absorbing though the details of babycare are, they are only the beginning . . .

Feeling tied down by motherhood

Well, it's a fact: you *are* tied down by motherhood! Whatever your previous commitments – job, mortgage, etc – they were probably none of them quite as unleavable as two children. One baby isn't quite the same – you can always hang on to the vague image of yourself setting off into the sunset with backpack and sling if the worst ever really came to the worst. But it doesn't take many weeks of life with two to dispel this one for good.

However, a growing family can provide a comforting structure within which to operate. You may in fact be content to be settled at last, not to be obliged to go hunting for pots of gold under the rainbow any more. Says Mary, mother of Johnnie and baby Rose:

> I feel that a second baby has made me grow up in a way that a first baby didn't. Because you are that much more committed, the inner changes you make with a second baby are that much deeper.

Other women do admit to feeling trapped:

Hilda for example found having two children very hard work. According to family legend, all the males of the clan were 'difficult' until they were two years old – and her own two boys Toby and Ben seemed to be running true to form! Hilda was especially irritated by the lack of freedom in little things. 'You could always make a quick run to the shops for a pint of milk with one child, but with two, it's hopeless. Either Ben will refuse to go in his pushchair, and scream the whole way, or Toby won't want to walk. By the time you've got them there, the shops are shut!'

However, she was a sociable girl who valued her circle of friends highly, or, as she puts it, 'Going out to tea keeps me sane!' Maybe too she secretly relished a difficult life, for she even admitted a hankering for a third baby!

Susan, who had always been a full-time mother, felt less able to make the transition from looking after one fairly independent child, to being on 24-hour call for a new baby again. She felt that any personal ambitions (even minor ones, like a private trip to the loo!) were being eroded by the demands of two children, and that it was just easier to knuckle down to the elimination of selfish concerns and play along for a quiet life. 'For quite a while, it didn't seem worth putting on nice clothes, because the kids would get them dirty. Going out was too much trouble, especially as they always slept in the car on the way back and then wouldn't go to bed on time'.

These feelings not unnaturally led to Susan being rather depressed, though not enough to need any treatment. Once the first year was over, Susan did feel the worst was over, and that she could take a new interest in life again in the form of a local school which ran a workshop for mothers.

You and your second baby

While struggling to get your other feelings into perspective, your growing relationship with your second baby is part of the centre of your life. One of the joys of second-time parenting is that, for many mothers, the initial period when you are constantly giving to the baby isn't as trying as first time round, because you know that the baby will be giving back ten-fold relatively soon. So, many mothers find they don't have to work as hard at this relationship; they're more content to accept the baby on his terms.

Often, part of this is not hurrying the second baby. Parents of a first child can be very eager to see her progress – sometimes even to the point of wishing her babyhood away as they impatiently await crawling, teething and other markers. It's an endless temptation to compare the first baby with babies down the road: 'Mrs Smith's baby sat up at four months and walked at ten!' This competitive edge, induced by inexperience and anxiety, is often lacking second-time round. Of course, this time you'll probably want to compare your second baby's progress to that of your first (if you can remember!) Accepting that your second baby is different from your first is one of the things which makes second-time motherhood so intrigueing. The second baby may be very different from the first, constantly baffling your expectations; even if she is very similar in some ways, she is still an individual. So, do try not to compare your two too much: 'she should be sleeping through by now – her sister was at her age,' is an obvious example of the kind of comparison which will only annoy you!

Three-month exhaustion

By three months, you will probably have settled down again after the upheaval of the birth. Maybe you will be returning to work, or at least in a frame of mind to take on more activities. This can be a dangerous time. Before you know it, the days have become crowded and you realize, belatedly, that you have taken too much on.

It may not actually be a matter of three months. Exhaustion can set in at any time – four, six or ten months after the birth. Many mothers go through a phase when, after a smoothish run, it all seems too much. Health may break down and life seems grey; there may be other signs of fatigue and stress such as poor sleeping, weepiness, irritability. Here is the time to look at your life and see if you are attempting too much, or if you feel under pressure of any kind.

It's worth noting that this can be quite minimal: doing too much varies very much from person to person and it may not always be something obvious, like having a job which involves 3 am calls to check the Hong Kong markets. Laura, for example, didn't realize that her almost daily visits to nearby friends were causing her a lot of stress. She invariably had to rush home for tea and would usually find the washing up waiting from lunch. Then came bathtime and bedtime for the children, for which she was usually in a bad mood. When she realized she (for her) was spending too much time out of the house, she was able to cut the outings down to three times a week.

Part of all this is the quite innocent refusal to accept the limitations of parenthood with two – or a wish to believe oneself stronger than one is! Of course, you do sometimes need to push yourself to the limit in order to find out what your limits are – but don't push too hard!

Time management

Whether or not you are earning money at work other than mothering, it makes sense to treat your time as a commodity so long as you are not too rigid about it. Flexibility is of the essence with a small family!

Time management typically starts with sorting out your priorities into urgent, not so urgent, and less urgent still. This can be difficult after a second baby because your priorities may be in such a state of flux, so try and look on the main idea of time management with two children as avoiding stress.

What are *your priorities?:* meals on time, clean clothes, sufficient shopping? One tidy room for adults only? Evenings free for yourself? The prospect of any of these may raise a wry smile if you're in the early days when to finish a breastfeed seems a positive luxury, but, whatever your aims, keep them fluid and don't set them too high. They will change from week to week.

Learn to pace yourself: do not take on too much. Look on time management not as the chance to get everything done if only you organize it well enough, but as a means of getting through the day in relative comfort.

Learn to say no: especially to other people who induce that gut-sinking feeling within you when they suggest a meeting!

Keep a noticeboard with pen affixed: to jot down reminders of anything important – post-natal amnesia does exist after second births, too!

Extra childcare

If you haven't organized anything before, do consider this now, even if you feel you don't need childcare because you're not doing paid work outside the home. If you can get your children cared for by someone else for even a morning, it can make the difference between bare survival and enjoyment.

If you feel you can't afford childcare, it is worth looking at your budget to see if there are any other economies you could make in order to pay a minder. It doesn't have to be an expensive qualified nanny – many local childminders charge much less and, as mothers themselves, are just as competent at looking after your children. Cut out the expensive biscuits and cakes which no one needs, and you may have enough money for a free morning!

12
Work

Having a second child can be a wonderfully releasing event. If like many women you feel that your second marks the end of your family, you may well feel at liberty to start afresh with life. A new phase is in the air, or at least round the corner. 'That's that out of the way – now on to something else!' is an inelegant way of putting it. You may now feel free to throw your energies back into work in a way that wasn't really possible while you were between pregnancies.

Two children can also act as a spur, inspiring you to feats you might otherwise not have attempted. Not only do they represent a family unit for which you need to provide economically; there is also the urge to live up to them, to work towards a status of which they might (one day!) be proud. For many, work is the most tangible manifestation of identity in their lives – something to point to when the children start to ask who you really are. Whether this should be so is another question, but society does tend to equate people's identities with what they do. This feeling seems to be especially true among fathers, who feel that their motives for working do become less ego-bound and more selfless with children.

While mothers who work of course value security for the children, they are also likely to appreciate self-fulfilment, an escape from the sometimes deadening monotony of family life, and a desire for independence and adult companionship.

Just as with the first baby, all these motivations have to be explored after your second birth – yet the pros and cons of returning to work this time are not exactly the same as before. It is harder to return to paid work after a second baby. This is for two main reasons. First, your childcare costs will double: this doesn't apply of course if you have been able to afford a nanny first-time round, who won't charge more for another child, but it is true of childminders, nurseries and crèches, and some women interpret this as a financial penalty for having children. Second, you are likely to be that much more tired because you are looking after two very small, demanding children, and may simply not have the energy or commitment for work. Third, if you worked first time round, you may feel that this time, you don't want to miss out on your baby, especially if you are planning for him/her to be your last.

Overall, some women find that, with another new member to the family, the temptation to remain at home is that much stronger. They may choose this time to give up work, even if they continued full- or part-time after their first birth.

Other mothers want to handle it differently. They may feel they had enough of looking after a baby the first time round. At this point, two or three years of being a mother can begin to feel like a long time. You may feel a longing for office gossip, uninterrupted hours at a typewriter, and samples of the latest fashions which a wage would bring. Or, you may miss the adrenalin which comes from working in a busy ward or shop. And, if you have some particular qualifications, you may be itching to use them again before they become totally rusty. After all, our education aims at equipping us for work rather than parenthood, and, no matter how strong our natural inclinations, it can be hard to do away with this conditioning.

A second birth can be frightening if you have always worked. All right, you got away with work and one child – just about – but are you still employable after two? Will you ever join the human race again? Some women are frankly horrified at how isolated they feel after a second birth, especially if they've managed to find some work that fitted in well with the demands of a first baby. With their identity as a working mother in jeopardy, they can't wait to get back to work and the 'real' world again!

Probably most people's feelings swing between these points and may remain ambivalent even after the choice has been made. Guilt is just as much a part of leaving two children for work as it is with one, as Hilda sadly noted one morning when she left her two with the childminder to go on to the hospital where she worked as a geriatric nurse:

> They were both crying – neither of them wanted to go, and I felt horrible. But the other part of me has to admit I was looking forward to six hours uninterrupted work. In some ways, my old ladies and gents are a doddle after two children!

Apart from the emotional reactions, the physical aspect of returning to work has to be considered and this is one area which

112

many women find difficult, particularly with full-time work. To get two children up and dressed is difficult at the best of times – how much more so early in the morning when everyone is sleepy and hurried, and the children have to be taken to the childminder's or the nursery on time. Likewise, it is hard to attend to everyone's needs in the evening state of general tiredness. Shopping still has to be done; housework has to be fitted in. With two children, parents who both work are likely to end up frankly exhausted!

However, that isn't the end of the story. The positive aspect of all this is increased appreciation of the times when the family is together. One teacher, who actually went on to do an MA degree when her second child was two, talks of how much they all enjoy weekends.

> Saturday is special – our day. We shop on Friday night, which is a struggle, but which leaves us the whole of the next day free, for outings or doing what we like. We do need my salary – we couldn't live on just my husband's – and any leftover money also means new clothes and holidays for us all. On balance, I prefer this way of life to scrimping and saving on one wage.

Childcare with two

Do you need to make any changes in your childcare with two children? If your first child is happily settled at a childminder's or nursery, you probably won't want to make any changes. And, even though you will be paying double, you may be able to work out some kind of money-saving 'package deal' with a small private nursery or a childminder that you've come to know well – not quite two for the price of one, but perhaps slightly less than the total cost of two full-time places.

There may be problems if you want the children to be together and lack of space makes it impossible; or you may feel that your child has grown out of her particular place of care. If you're not quite happy with your childcare, and want to make changes, you might want to consider someone coming to the house, rather than your children going out. Getting two ready to go out is much harder work than just one. In addition, you might well want more help with the housework. For this reason, probably the best option to

113

consider is a mother's help. (Make sure *all* her duties are fully understood before she starts work.) The only drawback with this is getting the house into some sort of order before she arrives – no matter what's in her contract she can't be expected to sort out a grade A mess every day. It depends on how untidy you and your toddler are! For more about how to choose a carer, ask your library for a good book (or see Further Reading).

With good, reliable childcare, there is no reason why you shouldn't go back to work after the statutory six months – some keen workers even go back before. It all depends on your commitment and energy level, but, if you pace yourself sensibly during the first six months of your second baby's life, you should be fit enough at least to give work a try.

Work: financially worthwhile?

For many women, the decision about whether to return to work after a second baby is made for them by economic considerations. No matter how little money their work may bring in after paying for childcare, they still need it in order to survive. For such women, it is one of life's harsher ironies that, just as the family needs more money, it becomes more difficult to earn it. If this is you, you may well feel infuriated at the way in which returning to work is so often discussed as if it were a *choice*, when in your case, necessity has eliminated that luxury. Or you may be relieved – at least *having* to work means less guilt at leaving the children!

Other women live on what statisticians would probably call borderline poverty, preferring to make adjustments in their style of living and to stay home and look after their children full time. Still others compromise and take on some form of part-time work to keep them 'ticking over', quite often at a level below their real ability because of the lowly nature of most part-time work. A few individuals manage successful jobshares. And still others create some form of paid work which they can do from home, with minimal childcare.

You may question whether returning to full-time work is really worth it, emotionally and financially, at a stage when your children need you so much, and childcare is so expensive and hard to arrange. In fact, only 18 per cent of mothers of very young children do work full time. And even those who say they need to, often need it for psychological reasons just as much as financial ones.

Samantha, who found a highly-pressurized publishing job when Anthony was three months old, insisted that they needed the money. However, she then went on to spend £400 on a new bed, and £200 on toys for the children, as well as more money on cushions, curtains and other assorted bits and pieces for their new home! When her husband John pointed out that she could spend less and stay at home, Samantha realized that the real reason she wanted to work was her sanity! 'I knew it would drive me mad to spend the whole day at home with the kids, much as I love them,' said she. Having just moved back to England from America, Samantha also realized that her spending was a way of putting down roots again in her native land, as well as gaining a clearer identity as a working mother of two.

Going back to work may be necessary for your peace of mind; it can also be seen as a long-term financial investment. If you want to keep your career going, it may be worth staying at work because you know that it will bring you more money and satisfaction later, even if childcare for two is swallowing your profits now.

Another way to count the financial costs is simply to divide them – mentally at least – between you and your partner. Don't look on it in terms of childcare absorbing all your wages, but half of yours, and half of his. Now how do you feel about the financial viability of returning to work?

Career decisions at this point are often a compromise between your own needs and those of your children, and women do often take on less-demanding posts than originally planned because of their family. One woman left the cut-and-thrust of a daily paper, where a 2 am call could summon her to cover a story anywhere in England, for the mellower atmosphere of a small monthly magazine. Another woman, a doctor who had at first been drawn to casualty work, decided instead to specialize in radiography because it meant a nine-to-five job.

Wages and childcare costs do of course vary enormously according to the type of job held, the hours worked, and the area you live in. You can pay anything from a quarter to the whole of your salary to whoever takes care of your children.

Sally, a teacher from Chatham, Kent, was lucky enough to find a small nursery which charged only a small amount per week per child – a quarter of her salary. She also had to pay a childminder an extra few pounds a week to drop them off and pick them up. The money left after tax, insurance and travel was the more necessary as her husband brought home far less a week as an employee in a local business.

Simone, who worked as a designer in central London, found she could expect to pay *at least* half her salary if not more for a full-time nursery place – for both children. The nursery was large and, she felt, overcrowded, a dumping place for parents who had to work. A full-time nanny would have cost even more – about three quarters of her salary. After childcare, tax, insurance and travel, she would have brought home very little. She decided not to work.

Annette, a London hospital physiotherapist, calculated that if she continued to work part-time with both children in the hospital crèche, she would be bringing home £4 a week – and so decided not to work!

The family budget: feeling poor

It has been estimated that it can cost as much as £42,000 to bring up a child to the age of 16. However, as stated before, small children aren't in themselves an expensive taste: it is the fact that they stop you working. It is generally recognized that those on the poverty line in the UK are all too often families with children. One survey found that the poorest quarter of the population were around 20 per cent poorer still if they had two children.

Although it is possible to spend hundreds or even thousands of pounds on clothes and equipment with a first baby this hardly applies to a second baby. You will of course have 'running costs' for both children – with the price of nappies and shoes favourite sources of complaint – but all in all, you won't have the expenditure that was necessary with a first baby.

Poverty, traditionally a Christian virtue, is today not generally seen as desirable. We also tend to compare with those better off than ourselves, not worse. It's a fact of human nature that thoughts of children in other parts of the world, who use rags for nappies and whose shoeless feet are riddled with tickworm, lose their force when we have to accept a decline in our own living standards. For some women, it's the worry about money in a consumer society, as much as actual lack of money, which can gnaw away at peace of mind. They may find it painful that they can't afford a private nursery; others find it hard work giving their children a healthy diet. Either way, it's important to make a distinction between being, and feeling, poor.

Certainly, one definition of poverty with two children can be an increased lack of freedom and independence at a time when you are already tied by motherhood. To take one high-class complaint, if you can't afford a car, it can be difficult to get out and see your friends, and galling to have them always visit you. You may feel that because you can't keep up economically, the friendships may have to go; as a result, you may feel increasingly isolated. (It is of course a fact of life that some friendships don't stand up to this sort of difficulty; or, that with the changes wrought by a second child, you might want to make new ones.)

We could probably all do with re-examining our values when a second child forces a lowering in lifestyle; we may be surprised at how much our self-esteem needs to be reflected by the material aspects of our lifestyles. It's true that being poor can impose a strain on yourself and your relationships, and adjusting to a drop in income can be demoralizing even if you aren't in actual need.

However, it is a peculiar sign of the times to consider whether we can 'afford' a second child, though this is a valid consideration for many parents. It isn't so much a question of what we will be able to give the child but of our expectations. Can we bear the stress of financial uncertainty if we decide to expand our family? It is worth being honest about this question, although unfortunately true honesty all too often comes only with the event! By the time you realize you can't 'afford' your second baby, he may be sitting there grinning at you from your threadbare kitchen rug!

Here are some suggestions for making ends meet:

- If you possibly can, do spend money on something you really need, like shoes or a new coat for your children. Otherwise, you waste emotional energy on struggling to make do without it – energy which could be put into saving or getting money in other ways.
- Don't skimp on food. Bulk-buying is often cheaper, so aim to do

117

a big shop (without the children) once a month. If you don't have a car, go with a friend and share petrol money, or take a taxi; one woman found she more than saved the fare by buying bigger sizes of everything. Take time to look for cheaper products which may not be at eye level; also for own brand products; prepackaged foods and ready-made meals are more costly.

- Check to see whether your gas and electricity bills are estimated (there will be an E on the bill). By reading the meter yourself you can sometimes save as much as £30!
- Look for free things to do with the children – parks, any local museums, any specific attractions (for example, in one area the local brewery was open on Sundays, with shire horses on view); read your local paper for school fêtes which often provide bouncing castles and other entertainment for minimal sums.
- Do try not to cultivate a 'poverty mentality' which involves always labelling yourself as poor. For example, don't get into the habit of saying, 'I can't afford to', the moment someone suggests spending money on goods or activities. You have to spend money sometimes!
- Keep a weekly budget – that way, you may be able to arrange it so that you do have spare money to spend, even if it's only a small sum. After budgeting for big items like mortgage, rent and heating bills, work out a reasonable sum with your partner for food and miscellaneous items such as medicine, stamps and tights and make sure you allot some to 'superfluous' activities.
- Check to see whether you are entitled to any state benefits; whether benefits would bring you in more money than working and paying a childminder; whether you could combine part-time work with some benefits.

Working from home

For many women, this is the ideal compromise. Working from home enables you to choose your own hours, and to organize your work around your children's needs and not vice-versa. Some people indeed see this way of working as a satisfying kind of return to pre-industrial conditions, when work and the family were far less separated than now.

Also, by the time you have a second child, you are so used to taking responsibility, that you may have moved away from the idea of being employed, and be ready to take the initiative and start something of your own.

Laura gave up teaching to start a family. When her second child Alicia was five months old, she started a private tutoring agency which she could run from home. Her initial costs involved buying an answerphone, stationary, and advertising. As a former teacher herself, Laura had a large bank of friends on which to draw for her teachers at first, many of them mothers like herself who were glad of the chance of earning a little extra money. Later, as the business expanded, Laura advertised for more teachers. 'I knew I didn't have the energy to go back into full-time teaching, this was something that could be done when I wanted – a lot of it takes place during the evenings when the children are asleep and teachers are at home.'

Alison, who went on to have a third child, started a book-keeping business with minimal costs for local advertising and stationary, which became highly successful. Having lost her previous job as a midwife, she was able to claim unemployment benefit and, later, a government enterprise allowance which was enough to cover her weekly childcare costs. She has this advice to give: 'If you've got an idea, do it! Having the nerve to go ahead is what's important!'

Liz, whose husband was made redundant, started selling her children's clothes at local car boot sales in order to make a little extra cash for shopping. This quickly proved so profitable that she was able to take a regular table at a local Friday market, and, later, a share in a shop with a friend who provided snacks and a play area for children.

What other ideas are there for starting to work from home? The options, it seems, are endless: all you need is one creative idea and a bit of confidence. Here are a few ideas from other women:

- Making curtains
- Making wooden toys
- Making jigsaws in the shape of people's names
- Selling jewellery

119

- Running a car boot stall
- Taking photos of children
- Decorating and selling home-made cakes
- Giving drama classes to children
- Organizing an hour of rhymes and songs for children
- Teaching children's tennis (short tennis)
- Teaching adults (French, Spanish, maths, music – anything)
- Setting up as an independent midwife
- Buying and restoring old furniture for re-sale
- Re-training in homeopathy and massage to do from home
- Setting up as a private physiotherapist
- Raising sheep and selling miniature ones made from their wool!
- Helping partner with his business as book-keeper, secretary.

If you feel like going ahead, do bear the following points in mind:

Start small: budget carefully for your initial costs – answerphone, stationary, perhaps separate phone line, materials, etc – as well as for the long-term expense of childcare.

Charge sensibly: even if you feel your work is done mainly for satisfaction rather than money, and keep clear accounts from the very start.

Consider an accountant: it may well save you money in the long run and fees can be offset against tax.

Set aside part of your profits: in a separate account in case they're needed later for tax.

Find out: whether you are entitled to any state allowances that might help you get your business off the ground.

Consider a loan: ask your bank, to cover initial cash flow problems. If you do, make sure you have a carefully drawn business plan to show him. While there, you can also ask his advice about your enterprise, even if you decide not to take it!

Confidence

Lack of confidence can be the only thing to stand between you and success. It is very easy to have a poor self-image as a second-time mother – because it may now be years since you worked, because you're so used to thinking of yourself as a mother, because you feel your clothes and hair aren't right, and so on. In fact, motherhood gives you many new skills as well as increased maturity, and just one piece of success can start you thinking more positively about yourself. So, how do you start?

- Take action – the first step towards something is often the hardest. Make that phone call, write that letter, book the class that might help towards your chosen work.
- Do one small thing at a time and don't try and foresee the results of what you do. You can't assess the value of your contribution in advance.
- Your physical state is very important in keeping confidence buoyed up – enough sleep, proper meals, walks in the open air, and breaks are all vital.
- Accept the truth about yourself: that you may be aiming too high or too low, that you do make mistakes. Being realistic is very comforting! Ask your partner or a close friend for feedback.
- Do make the effort to begin, but allow your work to gain its own momentum so you don't try too hard and then become discouraged and exhausted. For many mothers, real success is work that fits in comfortably with the realities of having two children.

Coda
The Future

Tales of woe abound in the lives of second-baby families – exhaustion, illness, and bad behaviour from adults and children alike. This book is not meant to be a cautionary tale, however, even if trying to tell the truth sometimes means walking a precarious line between reality and pessimism!

Parents with two children *do* have a future. This might seem like a bold statement in the face of the fact that, when you're in the early throes of life with two, any concept of the future mysteriously ceases to exist. Life has always been like this and always will be – a grey mêlée of early bedtimes and chronic fatigue, of uncontrollable scoldings and repentant cuddles, shot through with moments of delight like gleams of sunlight on a cloudy day. It's a life directed by a two-person team expert in the art of parental deflation, with your best sleep taken in three-hour chunks, snacks at the wrong times, naps at the wrong times, colds at the wrong times. If you're going through this now, rest assured: one day, life will open out again.

One year, we went to see some friends who were parents of a three- and a 20-month old. They were pleased to see us, but did not look entirely well: Linda in her old tracksuit looked pale, tense and underweight; Antonio seemed a bit strained. Over the lunch preparations Linda confided her feelings about being a mother of two. 'I feel like this', she said, showing me a clenched fist. Work – she was a full-time teacher – was a constant grind enlivened only by stressed relationships with colleagues; it barely brought in enough money for their needs. The cupboards in their house were bursting from the toys and clothes they had frantically thrown in earlier in the morning to make the place presentable. The meal took a long time to prepare: a chicken carved in careful, thin slices – for a treat, they told us. What conversation we had was continuously punctured by the children's interruptions. 'You do all the things you say you won't', said Linda above the phenomenal noise, guiltily handing them biscuits so they would let us talk for at least two minutes. As the parents of one child, we drove away with throbbing heads

122

and little true comprehension of our friends' plight. Around 18 months later, when our second baby was six months and our toddler two-and-a-half, Linda and Antonio came to see us one very blowy Boxing Day. This time it was different. The weather, which was keeping many people off the roads, didn't seem to bother them; we were touched they had driven so far to see us, especially as we didn't seem to see many people these days. Linda was resplendent in a new purple jumper and black slacks; Antonio wore good shoes and an ironed shirt. Above all, they exuded an air of relaxation, lounging in their armchairs while their delightful children, now that vital bit older, played in another room. They gave us impressive presents – ethnic silver jewellery and hand-made jigsaws for the children. They had brought half a splendid trifle left over from Christmas day; a crate of oranges. They had both had promotions at work; Linda had started a diploma, Antonio had taken up carving. 'But how thin you look,' they said to me, 'Are you well?' They had to help us arrange the turkey salad; there were so many things to wash and slice, it seemed an impossible undertaking to accomplish solo. We had totally forgotten any dessert; there was no festive cheer beyond a leftover quarter bottle of wine. Our tired baby cried but wouldn't sleep; my husband tried wheeling her out in the pushchair, only to be driven back by the force eight gale. Our toddler ran about naked. In another room, I wrestled with sellotape and used wrapping paper (needless to say we had none that was new) shamefacedly handing over our modest offerings: soap, socks for the children. Of course you don't judge a friendship by the size of the presents offered; it was the fact that, while they had obviously put some thought into choosing for us, we felt we had hardly bothered. In fact, we didn't seem to have made any preparation for their visit at all: no food ready, the house a mess, ourselves distracted. What could we have been about?

This transition from one state to another is hard to imagine in advance. But it does happen. One month you may find it impossible to think of going out because such beings as babysitters don't exist in your neighbourhood, and, anyway, you don't know when the baby's going to bed, the toddler refuses to go until the baby's asleep and, ideally, you would like to go to bed yourself at 8 pm! Next month, the girl next door has offered her services, the baby and the toddler have established a bedtime of 7.30-ish and you have the energy to keep going until 9 pm – just long enough to totter down to the new French restaurant along the road. But, no sooner have you taken your seat, than you are hit by new anxieties. What's going to happen next? Will the first child lead the way too much? Will the second child have too much of an easy run because your first child bears the brunt of all your disciplinary experiments? Will the second child develop what used to be called an inferiority complex from living in hand-me-downs? Are you reading enough to your second child or have you allowed yourself to burn out on a first-time run of Wee Willie Winkie and Pooh Bear?

These high-class problems should be gently put to one side while you probe the *entrecôte de maison*. Having got this far, the rest of it must be downhill. Don't take any notice of those parents who, asked if it's easier when the children are older, pull a wry face and say, 'The problems are different'. These people have forgotten what it was really like in the early days.

They only remember the good bits: how the toddler made 'stop crying noises' to comfort a distressed sibling; how the two of them made very sticky dough-and-water cakes together, and pigged themselves happily on the results; how the toddler would pull the baby away from a rabbit hutch in case the inmate decided to take a nip at his fingers; how the toddler would give the baby vocabulary lessons ('Say: sausages. Go on, say it! Say: pest'). How sweet they used to look asleep (finally) together in your bed, while your partner had crawled off to the sofa downstairs and you to the toddler's own bed . . .

But, while the children's togetherness is an indubitable part of what makes it all worthwhile, there is also the question of their separate characters and needs. How do you recognize and respond to the differences in your two? Are the years to come going to be haunted by the cry of 'It's not fair?' Do you have to be the judge with the scales poised equally all the time?

It's worth bearing in mind that, during the early years, the differences between the children are as much in terms of development as of personality: a newborn has different needs and behaviour to a three-year-old because of its age, not its character. In other words, it isn't really possible to be fair or unfair until the children are older and the younger child's needs have caught up with the older one's. And by then, you'll have learned more about the intrinsic differences between your children and will instinctively know how best to respond in the way that suits each individual best.

Some people can feel guilty because they find their feelings for one child are warmer than for the other. Parents do go through phases not so much of preferring one child to the other, but of finding one stage more enjoyable than the other. Some mothers love 18-month-olds; others feel more at ease when the four-year-mark has passed and you can converse with a semirational little being.

Whatever your feelings, it's true that parents have to be seen to be fair – but only up to a point. Striving for completely equal fairness implies that you can somehow have total control over your children's lives and reactions. Some injustices are best left to the children to resolve – even if you feel you can't bear them scrapping, it must teach them valuable conflict management skills!

There's also the practical aspect. When it comes to matters such as strictly equal turns on the swings, fairness is only a matter of counting the minutes. But how do you measure hugs? However, you can be fair in the spirit if not in the letter. The toddler who demands a taste of medicine because the teething baby has just wolfed down some junior paracetamol, may be just as happy with a biscuit. What's really at issue is acknowledgement; everyone likes a bit of recognition, and if it doesn't come in one form, it will be quite as welcome in another. In practice, you may be encouraged at how often a child will accept a compromise in the spirit in which it was offered!

This kind of adaptability could well be extended to the rest of life with two. It is so much easier if you can accept and appreciate what is going on right now. You don't have to sentimentalize after the event in order to enjoy second-time parenthood for what it is.

There are many privileges to watching two small lives unfold. It may be a matter of sharing the baby's first joke with the toddler, be it no more esoteric than a poke in the tummy. You have an excellent excuse for crawling back into bed with tea and biscuits when the people in the bunk beds favour a 5.45 am start to the day; and, after a while, they may even play together next door instead of coming to help you spread crumbs over the sheets.

The work imposed by two children gives you an unmissable chance to sort out your priorities and drop activities which you have always known to be good for you, like jogging, or trying to grow yoghurt, or reading the *Financial Times* from cover to cover every day. You will no longer wonder how people in power and top executives manage it; one of the most valuable gifts given by two children is the ability to keep going when anyone else would drop with exhaustion. After this, the most challenging work post will hold few terrors for you.

Neither will your children's general welfare. Your toddler will have taught you, albeit indirectly, that all tantrums end sometime. Having seen your toddler repeatedly survive temperatures of 103 will give you the confidence to take your baby to a chicken-pox party. You won't feel obliged to spend every Tuesday afternoon in the baby clinic because anyone can see that your second-born is putting on all the weight that could be required.

Most of all, after an initial struggle, you'll be able to enjoy a general relaxing of cares, engendered by the knowledge that your control will only stretch so far. You learn to take a pragmatic view of life, to interpret events to your own advantage. Does it really matter that, thanks to the toddler's initiative, both children are covered with that thick, white type of nappy cream which has to be removed with a spatula? At least it kept them happy for ten minutes while you had a rest.

You may even wonder at how much you've changed. Having two young children is a time of speedy evolution, even if it feels as if nothing much is happening outwardly. You need to integrate many changes in your life – with regard to both circumstances and attitudes, and it may help to remember this when you feel bored, or stressed.

Another point to remember is to use what free time you have for enjoyment, or even for doing nothing much. Wandering round the shops, reading an old Agatha Christie, or just sitting dreaming, can all provide valuable recovery points from a day spent in constant activity. Many mothers develop a habit of always doing something – or two things at once – so, practise doing very little sometimes in order to maintain a balance.

Perhaps some form of meditation can also help – pausing in your busy whirl to look at a sunset for two minutes, for example, or giving free rein to your thoughts in your bath, or listening to some music as you work. It doesn't have to be sitting cross-legged humming a mantra – just anything that you find spiritually refreshing. Paying this kind of attention to yourself will help keep you centred in a life where you as never before are the centre of many and varied demands.

Finally, an assortment of tips

Trivial though some of these points may seem, they can make all the difference as far as material and emotional tidiness are concerned.

For compulsive key-losers: organize your hall space. Put up a shelf or basket for keys and mail; another for junior shoes, combs, and any other items you normally need to mount a room-by-room hunt for when going out.

Keep a bag in the hall: packed with clothes and nappies for both children so you can just pick it up and leave when you want to go out.

Invest in more bins: as the house will be untidier, use one for each room – and train your toddler to put rubbish in. The baby will copy so check the bins before tipping out!

Help prevent toy squabbles: keep the toddler's special toys in a separate box out of the baby's reach, and their joint toys wherever they play most – kitchen, playroom or bedroom.

Buy one of each for both children: whether it's a lollipop or a vest, so they can't quarrel about preferential treatment!

Don't make the baby the excuse: for not doing what your toddler would like in terms of activities and outings.

Be very careful about labelling: the relationship between baby and toddler – 'They always fight in the bath' – as your children may live up to it! In fact, question *all* your assumptions about your children ('She's aggressive/he's shy') from time to time – give your children room to develop and change.

On a really frustrating day: drop everything and take them both out for a walk. If it's raining, have a blitz on the house instead – a clean room or two is wonderfully morale-boosting.

Get out of the house: on your own whenever the opportunity presents itself: create the opportunity if need be.

Continue to look after yourself: the way you did during pregnancy – an exhausted mother can't look after two children properly. Take plenty of vitamins and iron pills if you need them – have your haemoglobin level checked by your doctor if you fear you're anaemic. Eat as well as you can.

Keep your medicine cabinet: well stocked with basic supplies (check every few months for outdated stock.) Useful items are: (for you) pain relievers, cold cures, sore throat pastilles; (for the children) baby pain reliever, camomile cream for sore skin; for everyone, glucose and salt solutions for diarrhoea and tummy disorders, plasters, bandages, scissors, tweezers, antiseptic cream and/or solution.

Consider a lightweight umbrella buggy: If your old pushchair is becoming a bit decrepit a new model is relatively cheap and will make your life much easier.

Make sure your partner tidies up after himself: you will no longer have the time to do so yourself.

Cut down on clutter: be ruthless about disposing of clothes as soon as they're outworn, either in the attic or a charity shop. Don't buy too many new things at once, even when tempted by sales – stagger your spending to suit seasonal changes and growth in your children.

Don't be ashamed: of buying second-hand – later, you'll feel much happier about passing on items you didn't pay much for! Check the local paper, second-hand shops and fairs for items such as clothes, books and car seats (check equipment for safety.)

If you're finding life with two hard going: why not try starting up your own mothers' group? Advertise at your local library or doctor's surgery.

Do think about making a will: although it's a grim subject, and nominating friends or relatives to act as guardians for the children if you haven't already done so – just in case.

Don't torment yourself – with the responsibility of finding a solution to every problem of life with two – sometimes there isn't one immediately to hand. You can do your best with sleeping and squabbles, but sometimes it's just a question of gritting your teeth and going through it for a while until things change, either by your management or of their own accord.

Get to know your own limits.
Learn how to say no.

128

Further Reading

The Consumers Association. *Earning Money At Home*. 1989.

Douglas, Jo and Richman, Naomi. *My Child Won't Sleep*. Penguin Books, 1990.

Faber, Adele and Mazlish, Elaine. *Siblings without Rivalry*. Sidgwick & Jackson, 1989.

Fowler, Alan and Deborah. *Starting a Small Business*. Sphere Reference, 1990.

Hochschild, Arline. *The Second Shift*. Piatkus Books, 1990.

Moss, Peter and Brannen, Julia. *Managing Mothers*. Unwin Hyman, 1990.

Oppenheim, Carey. *Poverty: The Facts*. Child Poverty Action Group, 1990.

Schaefer, Charles E. and Petronko, Michael R. *Teach Your Baby to Sleep Through the Night*. Thorsons, 1989.

Pisani, Alison. *Sexual Problems in the Postnatal Period*. Unpublished paper.

Winston, Robert. *Getting Pregnant*. Anaya Publishers, 1990.

Useful Addresses

Association for Postnatal Illness (APNI) 25 Jerdan Place, London SW6 1BE. Tel: 071–731 4867 (10 am–2 pm).

Association of Radical Midwives 62 Greetby Hill, Ormskirk, Lancashire, L39 2DT. Tel: 0695 572776. Information on different types of natural childbirth.

Active Birth Centre 55 Dartmouth Park Road, London NW5 1SL. Tel: 071–267 3006. Offers classes on active birth.

British Pregnancy Advisory Service Head Office, Austy Manor, Wootton Wawen, Solihull, West Midlands, B95 6BX. Tel: 0564 793225. Advice on pregnancy.

Child PO Box 154, Hounslow, Middlesex, TW5 0EZ. Tel: 081–571 4367. Infertility self-help support group.

Contact a Family 16 Strutton Ground, London SW1P 2HP. Tel: 071–222 2695. For families of children with special needs and disabilities.

In Touch Trust 10 Norman Road, Sale, Cheshire M33 3DF. Tel: 061–962 4441. Information on all aspects of mental handicap.

La Lèche League BM 3424, London WC1N 3XX. Tel: 071–242 1278. Information and support on breastfeeding.

MENCAP (Royal Society for Mentally Handicapped Children and Adults), Mencap National Centre, 123 Golden Lane, London EC1Y 0RT. Tel: 071–454 0454.

MIND (National Association for Mental Health) 22 Harley Street, London W1N 2ED. Tel: 071–677 0741. Help with mental illness and with addiction to drugs like tranquillisers and anti-depressants.

The Miscarriage Association PO Box 24, Ossett, West Yorkshire, WF5 9XG. Tel: 0924 830515.

National Association for the Childless 318 Summer Lane, Birmingham, B19 3RL. Tel: 021–359 4887.

National Childbirth Trust (NCT) Alexandra House, Oldham Terrace, London W3 6NH. Tel: 081–992 8637.

RELATE: Marriage Guidance Council Head Office, Herbert Gray College, Little Church Street, Rugby CU21 3AP. Tel: 0788 573241.

Society to Support Home Confinements Lydgate, Wolsingham, Co Durham, DL13 3HA. Tel: 0388 528044 (after 6 pm).

The Whole Thing specializes in 'green' baby products, including cotton and wool nappies. For a free catalogue, contact them on: Tel: 0539 721922.

Index